Ballads

Miracle and Fyttes of Mirth

Popular Ballads of the Olden Times
Second Series

Frank Sidgwick

Alpha Editions

This edition published in 2021

ISBN : 9789354547218

Design and Setting By
Alpha Editions
www.alphaedis.com
Email - info@alphaedis.com

As per information held with us this book is in Public Domain.
This book is a reproduction of an important historical work. Alpha Editions uses the best technology to reproduce historical work in the same manner it was first published to preserve its original nature. Any marks or number seen are left intentionally to preserve its true form.

PREFACE

THE issue of this second volume of *Popular Ballads of the Olden Time* has been delayed chiefly by the care given to the texts, in most instances the whole requiring to be copied by hand.

I consider myself fortunate to be enabled, by the kind service of my friend Mr. A. Francis Steuart, to print for the first time in a collection of ballads the version of the *Grey Selchie of Shool Skerry* given in the Appendix. It is a feather in the cap of any ballad-editor after Professor Child to discover a ballad that escaped his eye.

My thanks are also due to the Rev. Professor W. W. Skeat for assistance generously given in connection with the ballad of *Judas*; and, as before, to Mr. A. H. Bullen.

F. S.

BALLADS IN THE SECOND SERIES

THE ballads in the present volume have been classified roughly so as to fall under the heads (i) Ballads of Superstition and of the Supernatural, including Dirges (pp. 1-122); (ii) Ballads of Sacred Origin (pp. 123-154); (iii) Ballads of Riddle and Repartee (pp. 155-181); and (iv) a few ballads, otherwise almost unclassifiable, collected under the title of 'Fyttes of Mirth,' or Merry Ballads (pp. 182 to end).

I

That the majority of the ballads in the first section are Scottish can hardly cause surprise. Superstition lurks amongst the mountains and in the corners of the earth. And, with one remarkable exception, all the best lyrical work in these ballads of the supernatural is to be found in the Scots. *Thomas Rymer, Tam Lin, The Wife of Usher's Well, Clerk Sanders,* and *The Dæmon Lover,* are perhaps the most notable examples amongst the ballads proper, and *Fair Helen of Kirconnell, The Twa Corbies,* and *Bonnie George Campbell* amongst the dirges. All these are known wherever poetry is read.

> 'For dulness, the creeping Saxons;
> For beauty and amorousness, the Gaedhills.'

But the exception referred to above, *The Unquiet Grave,* is true English, and yet lyrical, singing itself, like a genuine ballad, to a tune as one reads.

The complete superstition hinted at in this ballad should perhaps be stated more fully. It is obvious that excessive mourning is fatal to the peace of the dead; but it is also to be noticed that it is almost equally fatal to the mourner. The mourner in *The Unquiet Grave* is refused the kiss demanded, as it will be fatal. *Clerk Sanders,* on the other hand, has lost—if ever it possessed—any trace of this doctrine. For Margret does not die; though she would have died had she kissed him, we notice, and the kiss was demanded by her and refused by him: and Clerk Sanders is only disturbed in his grave because he has not got back his troth-plight. The method of giving this back—the stroking of a wand—we have had before in *The Brown Girl* (First Series, pp. 60-62, st. 14).

In the Helgi cycle of Early Western epics (*Corpus Poeticum Boreale,* vol. i. pp. 128 ff.), Helgi the hero is slain, and returns as a ghost to his lady, who follows him to his grave. But her tears are bad for him: they fall in blood on his corpse.

The subject of the Lyke-wake would easily bear a monograph to itself, and at present I know of none. I have therefore ventured, in choosing Aubrey's version in place of the better known one printed—and doubtless written over—by Sir Walter Scott, to give rather fuller information concerning the Dirge, its folklore, and its bibliography. A short study of the ramifications of the various superstitions incorporated therein leads to a sort of surprise that there is no popular ballad treating of the subject of St. Patrick's Purgatory, which has attracted more than one English poet. Thomas Wright's volume on the subject, however, is delightful and instructive reading.

II

The short section of Ballads of Sacred Origin contains all that we possess in England—notice that only two have Scottish variants, even fragmentary—and somewhat more than can be classified as ballads with strictness. Yet I would fain have added other of our 'masterless' carols, which to-day seem to survive chiefly in the West of England. One of their best lovers, Mr. Quiller-Couch, has complained that, after promising himself to include a representative selection of carols in his anthology, he was chagrined to discover that they lost their quaint delicacy when placed among other more artificial lyrics. Perhaps they would have been more at home set amongst these ballads; but I have excluded them with the less regret in remembering that they stand well alone in the collections of Sylvester, Sandys, Husk; in the reprints of Thomas Wright; and, in more recent years, in the selections of Mr. A. H. Bullen and Canon Beeching.

The Maid and the Palmer would appear to be the only ballad of Christ's wanderings on the earth that we possess, just as *Brown Robyn's Confession* is the only one of the miracles of the Virgin. One may guess, however, that others have descended rapidly into nursery rhymes, as in the case of one, noted in J. O. Halliwell's collection, which, in its absence, may be called *The Owl, or the Baker's Daughter*. For Ophelia knew that they said the owl was the baker's daughter. And the story of her metamorphosis is exactly paralleled by the Norse story of *Gertrude's Bird*, translated by Dasent.

Gertrude was an old woman with a red mutch on her head, who was kneading dough, when Christ came wandering by, and asked for a small bannock. Gertrude took a niggardly pinch of dough, and began to roll it into a bannock; but as she rolled, it grew, until she put it aside as too large to give away, and took a still smaller pinch. This also grew miraculously, and was put aside. The same thing happened a third time, till she said, 'I cannot roll you a small bannock.' Then Christ said, 'For your selfishness, you shall become a bird, and seek your food 'twixt bark and bole.' Gertrude at once became a bird, and flew up into a tree with a screech. And to this day the great woodpecker of Scandinavia is called 'Gertrude's Bird,' and has a red head.

III

The Ballads of Riddle and Repartee do not amount to very many in our tongue. But they contain riddles which may be found in one form or another in nearly every folklore on the earth. Even Samson had a riddle. Always popular, they seem to have been especial favourites in early Oriental literature, in the mediæval Latin races, and, in slightly more modern times, amongst the Teutonic and Scandinavian peoples. Perhaps *King John and the Abbot* is the best English specimen, for it is to-day as pleasing to an audience as it can ever have been. But *Lady Isabel and the Elf Knight*, better known as *May Colvin*, is the most startling of any, in its myriad ramifications and supposed origin.

IV

The 'Fyttes of Mirth' conclude the present volume. It may be as well to say here that I have placed under this head any ballad that tells of a successful issue and has a happy ending or mirthful climax.

The version I have given of that famous ballad *The Lord of Learne* (or, more commonly, *Lorne*) is most enchanting in its *naïveté*, and, when read aloud or recited, is exceedingly effective. The curious remark that the affectionate parting between the young Lord and his father and mother would have changed even a Jew's heart; the picturesque description of the siege of the castle, so close that 'a swallow could not have flown away'; the sudden descent from romance to a judicial trial; the remarkable assumption by the foreman of the jury of the privileges of a judge; and the thoroughly satisfactory description of the false steward's execution—

'I-wis they did him curstly cumber!'

—all these help to form the ever-popular *Lord of Learne*.

The remaining 'Fyttes of Mirth' are mostly well known, and require no further comment.

ADDITION TO GLOSSARY OF BALLAD COMMONPLACES

(See First Series, pp. xlvi-li)

THE late Professor York Powell explained to me, since the note on 'gare' (First Series, p. 1) was written, that the word means exactly what is meant by 'gore' in modern dressmaking. The antique skirt was made of four pieces: two cut square, to form the front and the back; and two of a triangular shape, to fill the space between, the apex of the triangle, of course, being at the waist. Thus a knife that 'hangs low down' by a person's 'gare,' simply means that the knife hung at the side and not in front.

THOMAS RYMER

THE TEXT.—The best-known text of this famous ballad is that given by Scott in the *Minstrelsy of the Scottish Border*, derived 'from a copy obtained from a lady residing not far from Erceldoune, corrected and enlarged by one in Mrs. Brown's MS.' Scott's ballad is compounded, therefore, of a traditional version, and the one here given, from the Tytler-Brown MS., which was printed by Jamieson with a few changes. It does not mention Huntlie bank or the Eildon tree. Scott's text may be seen printed parallel with Jamieson's in Professor J. A. H. Murray's book referred to below.

THE STORY.—As early as the fourteenth century there lived a Thomas of Erceldoune, or Thomas the Rhymer, who had a reputation as a seer and prophet. His fame was not extinct in the nineteenth century, and a collection of prophecies by him and Merlin and others, first issued in 1603, could be found at the beginning of that century 'in most farmhouses in Scotland' (Murray, *The Romance and Prophecies of Thomas of Erceldoune*, E.E.T.S., 1875). The existence of a Thomas de Ercildoun, son and heir of Thomas Rymour de Ercildoun, both living during the thirteenth century, is recorded in contemporary documents.

A poem, extant in five manuscripts (all printed by Murray as above), of which the earliest was written about the middle of the fifteenth century, relates that Thomas of Erceldoune his prophetic powers were given him by the Queen of Elfland, who bore him away to her country for some years, and then restored him to this world lest he should be chosen for the tribute paid to hell. So much is told in the first fytte, which corresponds roughly to our ballad. The rest of the poem consists of prophecies taught to him by the Queen.

The poem contains references to a still earlier story, which probably narrated only the episode of Thomas's adventure in Elfland, and to which the prophecies of Thomas Rymour of Ercildoun were added at a later date. The story of Thomas and the Queen of Elfland is only another version of a legend of Ogier le Danois and Morgan the Fay.

Our ballad is almost certainly derived directly from the poem, and the version here given is not marred by the repugnant ending of Scott's ballad, where Thomas objects to the gift of a tongue that can never lie. But Scott's version retains Huntlie bank and the Eildon tree, both mentioned in the old poem, and both exactly located during last century at the foot of the Eildon Hills, above Melrose (see an interesting account in Murray, *op. cit.*, Introduction, pp. l-lii and footnotes).

THOMAS RYMER

1.
    TRUE Thomas lay o'er yond grassy bank,
    And he beheld a ladie gay,
    A ladie that was brisk and bold,
    Come riding o'er the fernie brae.

2.
    2.³ 'tett,' lock or bunch of hair.
    Her skirt was of the grass-green silk,
    Her mantel of the velvet fine,
    At ilka tett of her horse's mane
    Hung fifty silver bells and nine.

3.
    True Thomas he took off his hat,
    And bowed him low down till his knee:
    'All hail, thou mighty Queen of Heaven!
    For your peer on earth I never did see.'

4.
    'O no, O no, True Thomas,' she says,
    'That name does not belong to me;
    I am but the queen of fair Elfland,
    And I'm come here for to visit thee.

5.
    'But ye maun go wi' me now, Thomas,
    True Thomas, ye maun go wi' me,
    For ye maun serve me seven years,
    Thro' weel or wae, as may chance to be.'

6.
    She turned about her milk-white steed,
    And took True Thomas up behind,
    And aye whene'er her bridle rang,
    The steed flew swifter than the wind.

7.
    7 is 15 in the MS.
    For forty days and forty nights
    He wade thro' red blude to the knee,
    And he saw neither sun nor moon,
    But heard the roaring of the sea.

8.
> 8.² 'garden': '*golden green*, if my copy is right.' —CHILD.
> O they rade on, and further on,
> Until they came to a garden green:
> 'Light down, light down, ye ladie free,
> Some of that fruit let me pull to thee.'

9.
> 'O no, O no, True Thomas,' she says,
> 'That fruit maun not be touched by thee,
> For a' the plagues that are in hell
> Light on the fruit of this countrie.

10.
> 'But I have a loaf here in my lap,
> Likewise a bottle of claret wine,
> And now ere we go farther on,
> We'll rest a while, and ye may dine.'

11.
> 11.⁴ 'fairlies,' marvels.
> When he had eaten and drunk his fill;
> 'Lay down your head upon my knee,'
> The lady sayd, 'ere we climb yon hill,
> And I will show you fairlies three.

12.
> 'O see not ye yon narrow road,
> So thick beset wi' thorns and briers?
> That is the path of righteousness,
> Tho' after it but few enquires.

13.
> 13.² 'lillie leven,' smooth lawn set with lilies.
> 'And see not ye that braid braid road,
> That lies across yon lillie leven?
> That is the path of wickedness,
> Tho' some call it the road to heaven.

14.
> 'And see not ye that bonny road,
> Which winds about the fernie brae?
> That is the road to fair Elfland,
> Where you and I this night maun gae.

15.
> 'But, Thomas, ye maun hold your tongue,
> Whatever you may hear or see,
> For gin ae word you should chance to speak,
> You will ne'er get back to your ain countrie.'

16.
> 16.[1] 'even cloth,' cloth with the nap worn off.
> He has gotten a coat of the even cloth,
> And a pair of shoes of velvet green,
> And till seven years were past and gone
> True Thomas on earth was never seen.

THE QUEEN OF ELFAN'S NOURICE

THE TEXT.—As printed in Sharpe's Ballad Book, from the Skene MS. (No. 8). It is fragmentary—regrettably so, especially as stanzas 10-12 belong to *Thomas Rymer*.

THE STORY is the well-known one of the abduction of a young mother to be the Queen of Elfland's nurse. Fairies, elves, water-sprites, and nisses or brownies, have constantly required mortal assistance in the nursing of fairy children. Gervase of Tilbury himself saw a woman stolen away for this purpose, as she was washing clothes in the Rhone.

The genuineness of this ballad, deficient as it is, is best proved by its lyrical nature, which, as Child says, 'forces you to chant, and will not be read.'

'Elfan,' of course, is Elfland; 'nourice,' a nurse.

THE QUEEN OF ELFAN'S NOURICE

1.
    1.⁴ 'ben,' within.
    'I HEARD a cow low, a bonnie cow low,
    An' a cow low down in yon glen;
    Lang, lang, will my young son greet
    Or his mother bid him come ben.

2.
    'I heard a cow low, a bonnie cow low,
    An' a cow low down in yon fauld;
    Lang, lang will my young son greet
    Or his mither take him frae cauld.
      *   *   *   *   *

3.
    Waken, Queen of Elfan,
    An' hear your nourice moan.'

4.
    'O moan ye for your meat,
    Or moan ye for your fee,
    Or moan ye for the ither bounties
    That ladies are wont to gie?'

5.
    'I moan na for my meat,
    Nor moan I for my fee,

Nor moan I for the ither bounties
That ladies are wont to gie.

6.
'. . . . .
. . . . .

But I moan for my young son
I left in four nights auld.

7.
'I moan na for my meat,
Nor yet for my fee,
But I mourn for Christen land,
It's there I fain would be.'

8.
'O nurse my bairn, nourice,' she says,
'Till he stan' at your knee,
An' ye's win hame to Christen land,
Whar fain it's ye wad be.

9.
9.² *i.e.* till he can walk by holding on to things.
'O keep my bairn, nourice,
Till he gang by the hauld,
An' ye's win hame to your young son
Ye left in four nights auld.'

* * * * *

10.
'O nourice lay your head
Upo' my knee:
See ye na that narrow road
Up by yon tree?

11.
. . . . .
. . . . .

That's the road the righteous goes,
And that's the road to heaven.

12.
'An' see na ye that braid road,
Down by yon sunny fell?
Yon's the road the wicked gae,
An' that's the road to hell.'

ALLISON GROSS

THE TEXT is that of the Jamieson-Brown MS.

THE STORY is one of the countless variations of the French 'Beauty and the Beast.' A modern Greek tale narrates that a nereid, enamoured of a youth, and by him scorned, turned him into a snake till he should find another love as fair as she.

The feature of this ballad is that the queen of the fairies should have power to undo the evil done by a witch.

ALLISON GROSS

1.
>O ALLISON GROSS, that lives in yon tow'r,
>The ugliest witch i' the north country,
>Has trysted me ae day up till her bow'r,
>An' monny fair speech she made to me.

2.
>She stroaked my head, an' she kembed my hair,
>An' she set me down saftly on her knee;
>Says, 'Gin ye will be my lemman so true,
>Sae monny braw things as I woud you gi'.'

3.
>She show'd me a mantle o' red scarlet,
>Wi' gouden flow'rs an' fringes fine;
>Says, 'Gin ye will be my lemman sae true,
>This goodly gift it sal be thine.'

4.
>'Awa', awa', ye ugly witch,
>Haud far awa', an' lat me be;
>I never will be your lemman sae true,
>An' I wish I were out o' your company.'

5.
>5.[1] 'sark,' shirt.
>She neist brought a sark o' the saftest silk,
>Well wrought wi' pearles about the ban';
>Says, 'Gin ye will be my ain true love,
>This goodly gift you sal comman'.'

6.
>She show'd me a cup o' the good red gold,

Well set wi' jewls sae fair to see;
Says, 'Gin you will be my lemman sae true,
This goodly gift I will you gi'.'

7.

'Awa', awa', ye ugly witch,
Had far awa', and lat me be!
For I woudna ance kiss your ugly mouth
For a' the gifts that you coud gi'.'

8.

She's turn'd her right and roun' about,
An' thrice she blaw on a grass-green horn;
An' she sware by the meen and the stars abeen,
That she'd gar me rue the day I was born.

9.

Then out has she ta'en a silver wand,
An' she's turn'd her three times roun' and roun';
She's mutter'd sich words till my strength it fail'd,
An' I fell down senceless upon the groun'.

10.

She's turn'd me into an ugly worm,
And gard me toddle about the tree;
An' ay, on ilka Saturday's night,
My sister Maisry came to me;

11.

Wi' silver bason and silver kemb,
To kemb my heady upon her knee;
But or I had kiss'd her ugly mouth,
I'd rather 'a' toddled about the tree.

12.

12.² 'the seely court,' *i.e.* the fairies' court.
12.³ 'gowany,' daisied.
But as it fell out on last Hallow-even,
When the seely court was ridin' by,
The queen lighted down on a gowany bank,
Nae far frae the tree where I wont to lye.

13.

She took me up in her milk-white han',
An' she's stroak'd me three times o'er her knee;
She chang'd me again to my ain proper shape,
And I nae mair maun toddle about the tree.

THE LAILY WORM AND THE MACHREL OF THE SEA

THE TEXT of this mutilated ballad is taken from the Skene MS., where it was written down from recitation in the North of Scotland about 1802.

THE STORY is of a double transformation of a sister and brother by a stepmother. Compare the story of *The Marriage of Sir Gawaine* (First Series, p. 108). *Allison Gross* should be compared closely with this ballad. The combing of hair seems to be a favourite method of expressing affection, not only in these ballads, but also in Scandinavian folklore. It is needless to take exception to the attribution either of hair to a worm, or of knees to a machrel: though we may note that in one version of *Dives and Lazarus* Dives 'has a place prepared in hell to sit on a serpent's knee.' However, it is probable that a part of the ballad, now lost, stated that the machrel (whatever it may be) reassumed human shape 'every Saturday at noon.'

THE LAILY WORM AND THE MACHREL OF THE SEA

1.
    'I was but seven year auld
    When my mither she did die;
    My father married the ae warst woman
    The warld did ever see.

2.
    2.[1] etc. 'laily' = laidly, loathly.
    'For she has made me the laily worm,
    That lies at the fit o' the tree,
    An' my sister Masery she's made
    The machrel of the sea.

3.
    'An' every Saturday at noon
    The machrel comes to me,
    An' she takes my laily head
    An' lays it on her knee,
    She kaims it wi' a siller kaim,
    An' washes 't in the sea.

4.
    'Seven knights hae I slain,
    Sin I lay at the fit of the tree,

        An' ye war na my ain father,
        The eight ane ye should be.'

5.
        'Sing on your song, ye laily worm,
        That ye did sing to me:'
        'I never sung that song but what
        I would sing it to thee.

6.
        'I was but seven year auld,
        When my mither she did die;
        My father married the ae warst woman
        The warld did ever see.

7.
        'For she changed me to the laily worm,
        That lies at the fit o' the tree,
        And my sister Masery
        To the machrel of the sea.

8.
        'And every Saturday at noon
        The machrel comes to me,
        An' she takes my laily head
        An' lays it on her knee,
        An' kames it wi' a siller kame,
        An' washes it i' the sea.

9.
        'Seven knights hae I slain
        Sin I lay at the fit o' the tree;
        An' ye war na my ain father,
        The eighth ane ye shoud be.'

10.
        He sent for his lady,
        As fast as send could he:
        'Whar is my son that ye sent frae me,
        And my daughter, Lady Masery?'

11.
        'Your son is at our king's court,
        Serving for meat an' fee,
        An' your daughter's at our queen's court,
        .   .   .   .   .'

12.
        'Ye lie, ye ill woman,
        Sae loud as I hear ye lie;
        My son's the laily worm,

  That lies at the fit o' the tree,
  And my daughter, Lady Masery,
  Is the machrel of the sea!'

13.
  She has tane a siller wan',
  An' gi'en him strokes three,
  And he has started up the bravest knight
  That ever your eyes did see.

14.
  She has ta'en a small horn,
  An' loud an' shrill blew she,
  An' a' the fish came her untill
  But the proud machrel of the sea:
  'Ye shapeit me ance an unseemly shape,
  An' ye's never mare shape me.'

15.
  He has sent to the wood
  For whins and for hawthorn,
  An' he has ta'en that gay lady,
  An' there he did her burn.

KEMP OWYNE

THE TEXT is that given (nearly *literatim*) by Buchan and Motherwell, and also in the MSS. of the latter.

THE STORY.—This adventure of Owyne (Owain, 'the King's son Urien,' Ywaine, etc.), with the subsequent transformation, has a parallel in an Icelandic saga. Rehabilitation in human shape by means of a kiss is a common tale in the Scandinavian area; occasionally three kisses are necessary.

A similar ballad, now lost, but re-written by the contributor, from scraps of recitation by an old woman in Berwickshire, localises the story of the firedrake ('the laidly worm') near Bamborough in Northumberland; and Kinloch said that the term 'Childe o' Wane' was still applied by disconsolate damsels of Bamborough to any youth who champions them. However, Mr. R. W. Clark of Bamborough, who has kindly made inquiries for me, could find no survival of this use.

The ballad is also called 'Kempion.'

KEMP OWYNE

1.
HER mother died when she was young,
Which gave her cause to make great moan;
Her father married the warst woman
That ever lived in Christendom.

2.
She served her with foot and hand,
In every thing that she could dee,
Till once, in an unlucky time,
She threw her in ower Craigy's sea.

3.
3.³ 'Kemp' = champion, knight. Cp. 'Childe' in *Childe Maurice*, etc.
3.⁴ 'borrow,' ransom.
Says, 'Lie you there, dove Isabel,
And all my sorrows lie with thee;
Till Kemp Owyne come ower the sea,
And borrow you with kisses three,
Let all the warld do what they will,
Oh borrowed shall you never be!'

4.
> Her breath grew strang, her hair grew lang,
> And twisted thrice about the tree,
> And all the people, far and near,
> Thought that a savage beast was she.

5.
> These news did come to Kemp Owyne,
> Where he lived, far beyond the sea;
> He hasted him to Craigy's sea,
> And on the savage beast look'd he.

6.
> Her breath was strang, her hair was lang,
> And twisted was about the tree,
> And with a swing she came about:
> 'Come to Craigy's sea, and kiss with me.

7.
> 'Here is a royal belt,' she cried,
> 'That I have found in the green sea;
> And while your body it is on,
> Drawn shall your blood never be;
> But if you touch me, tail or fin,
> I vow my belt your death shall be.'

8.
> He stepped in, gave her a kiss,
> The royal belt he brought him wi';
> Her breath was strang, her hair was lang,
> And twisted twice about the tree,
> And with a swing she came about:
> 'Come to Craigy's sea, and kiss with me.

9.
> 'Here is a royal ring,' she said,
> 'That I have found in the green sea;
> And while your finger it is on,
> Drawn shall your blood never be;
> But if you touch me, tail or fin,
> I swear my ring your death shall be.'

10.
> He stepped in, gave her a kiss,
> The royal ring he brought him wi';
> Her breath was strang, her hair was lang,
> And twisted ance about the tree,
> And with a swing she came about:
> 'Come to Craigy's sea, and kiss with me.

11.
      'Here is a royal brand,' she said,
      'That I have found in the green sea;
      And while your body it is on,
      Drawn shall your blood never be;
      But if you touch me, tail or fin,
      I swear my brand your death shall be.'

12.
      He stepped in, gave her a kiss,
      The royal brand he brought him wi';
      Her breath was sweet, her hair grew short,
      And twisted nane about the tree,
      And smilingly she came about,
      As fair a woman as fair could be.

WILLIE'S LADY

THE TEXT is from the lost Fraser-Tytler-Brown MS., this ballad luckily having been transcribed before the MS. disappeared. Mrs. Brown recited another and a fuller version to Jamieson.

THE STORY.—Willie's mother, a witch, displeased at her son's choice, maliciously arrests by witchcraft the birth of Willie's son. Willie's travailing wife sends him again and again to bribe the witch, who refuses cup, steed, and girdle. Here our version makes such abrupt transitions, that it will be well to explain what takes place. The Belly Blind or Billie Blin (see *Young Bekie*, First Series, pp. 6, 7) advises Willie to make a sham baby of wax, and invite his witch-mother to the christening. Willie does so (in stanzas lost between our 33 and 34); the witch, believing the wax-baby to be flesh and blood, betrays all her craft by asking who has loosed the knots, ta'en out the kaims, ta'en down the woodbine, etc., these being the magic rites by which she has suspended birth. Willie instantly looses the knots and takes out the kaims, and his wife presents him with a bonny young son.

The story is common in Danish ballads, and occasional in Swedish. In the classics, Juno (Hera) on two occasions delayed childbirth and cheated Ilithyia, the sufferers being Latona and Alcmene. But the latest version of the story is said to have occurred in Arran in the nineteenth century. A young man, forsaking his sweetheart, married another maiden, who when her time came suffered exceedingly. A packman who chanced to be passing heard the tale and suspected the cause. Going to the discarded sweetheart, he told her that her rival had given birth to a fine child; thereupon she sprang up, pulled a large nail out of the beam, and called to her mother, 'Muckle good your craft has done!' The labouring wife was delivered forthwith. (See *The Folklore Record*, vol. ii. p. 117.)

WILLIE'S LADY

1.
>WILLIE has taen him o'er the fame,
>He's woo'd a wife and brought her hame.

2.
>He's woo'd her for her yellow hair,
>But his mother wrought her mickle care,

3.
>And mickle dolour gard her dree,
>For lighter she can never be.

4.
>But in her bower she sits wi' pain,
>And Willie mourns o'er her in vain.

5.
>And to his mother he has gone,
>That vile rank witch of vilest kind.

6.
>He says: 'My ladie has a cup
>Wi' gowd and silver set about.

7.
>'This goodlie gift shall be your ain,
>And let her be lighter o' her young bairn.'

8.
>'Of her young bairn she'll ne'er be lighter,
>Nor in her bower to shine the brighter.

9.
>'But she shall die and turn to clay,
>And you shall wed another may.'

10.
>'Another may I'll never wed,
>Another may I'll ne'er bring home.'

11.
>But sighing says that weary wight,
>'I wish my life were at an end.'

12.
>'Ye doe [ye] unto your mother again,
>That vile rank witch of vilest kind.

13.
>'And say your ladie has a steed,
>The like o' 'm's no in the lands of Leed.

14.
>'For he's golden shod before,
>And he's golden shod behind.

15.
>'And at ilka tet of that horse's main
>There's a golden chess and a bell ringing.

16.
>'This goodlie gift shall be your ain,
>And let me be lighter of my young bairn.'

17.
>'O' her young bairn she'll ne'er be lighter,
>Nor in her bower to shine the brighter.

18.

19.
    'But she shall die and turn to clay,
    And ye shall wed another may.'

19 'I'll' is 'I' in both lines in the MS.

20.
    'Another may I'll never wed,
    Another may I'll neer bring hame.'

21.
    But sighing said that weary wight,
    'I wish my life were at an end.'

22.
    'Ye doe [ye] unto your mother again,
    That vile rank witch of vilest kind.

23.
    'And say your ladie has a girdle,
    It's red gowd unto the middle.

24.
    'And ay at every silver hem
    Hangs fifty silver bells and ten.

24.[1] 'sall' is Scott's emendation for *has* in the MS.

25.
    'That goodlie gift sall be her ain,
    And let me be lighter of my young bairn.'

26.
    'O' her young bairn she's ne'er be lighter,
    Nor in her bower to shine the brighter.

27.
    'But she shall die and turn to clay,
    And you shall wed another may.'

28.
    'Another may I'll never wed,
    Another may I'll ne'er bring hame.'

29.
    But sighing says that weary wight,
    'I wish my life were at an end.'

30.
    Then out and spake the Belly Blind;
    He spake aye in good time.

31.
    'Ye doe ye to the market place,
    And there ye buy a loaf o' wax.

    'Ye shape it bairn and bairnly like,
    And in twa glassen een ye pit;

32.
    'And bid her come to your boy's christening;
    Then notice weel what she shall do.
33.
    'And do you stand a little forebye,
    And listen weel what she shall say.'
    *   *   *   *   *
34.
    'O wha has loosed the nine witch knots
    That was amo' that ladie's locks?
35.
    'And wha has taen out the kaims of care
    That hangs amo' that ladie's hair?
36.
    'And wha's taen down the bush o' woodbine
    That hang atween her bower and mine?
37.
    'And wha has kill'd the master kid
    That ran beneath that ladie's bed?
38.
    'And wha has loosed her left-foot shee,
    And lotten that lady lighter be?'
39.
    O Willie has loosed the nine witch knots
    That was amo' that ladie's locks.
40.
    And Willie's taen out the kaims o' care
    That hang amo' that ladie's hair.
41.
    And Willie's taen down the bush o' woodbine
    That hang atween her bower and thine.
42.
    And Willie has killed the master kid
    That ran beneath that ladie's bed.
43.
    And Willie has loosed her left-foot shee,
    And letten his ladie lighter be.
44.
    And now he's gotten a bonny young son,
    And mickle grace be him upon.

THE WEE WEE MAN

THE TEXT is that of Herd's MS. and his *Scots Songs*. Other versions vary very slightly, and this is the oldest of them.

There is a fourteenth-century MS. (in the Cotton collection) containing a poem not unlike *The Wee Wee Man*; but there is no justification in deriving the ballad from the poem, which may be found in Ritson's *Ancient Songs* (1829), i. p. 40.

Scott incorporates the story with *The Young Tamlane*.

THE WEE WEE MAN

1.
> 1.[4] 'ere,' *i.e.* e'er.
> As I was wa'king all alone,
> Between a water and a wa',
> And there I spy'd a wee wee man,
> And he was the least that ere I saw.

2.
> 2.[1] 'shathmont,' a span.
> 2.[2] 'thimber,' gross.
> His legs were scarce a shathmont's length,
> And thick and thimber was his thigh;
> Between his brows there was a span,
> And between his shoulders there was three.

3.
> He took up a meikle stane,
> And he flang 't as far as I could see;
> Though I had been a Wallace wight,
> I couldna liften't to my knee.

4.
> 'O wee wee man, but thou be strang!
> O tell me where thy dwelling be?'
> 'My dwelling's down at yon bonny bower;
> O will you go with me and see?'

5.
> On we lap, and awa' we rade,
> Till we came to yon bonny green;
> We lighted down for to bait our horse,
> And out there came a lady fine.

6.
>   Four and twenty at her back,
>   And they were a' clad out in green;
>   Though the King of Scotland had been there,
>   The warst o' them might hae been his queen.

7.
>   On we lap, and awa' we rade,
>   Till we came to yon bonny ha',
>   Whare the roof was o' the beaten gould,
>   And the floor was o' the cristal a'.

8.
>   When we came to the stair-foot,
>   Ladies were dancing, jimp and sma',
>   But in the twinkling of an eye,
>   My wee wee man was clean awa'.

COSPATRICK

THE TEXT is that of Scott's *Minstrelsy* (1802). It was 'taken down from the recitation of a lady' (his mother's sister, Miss Christian Rutherford), and collated with a copy in the Tytler-Brown MS. The ballad is also called *Gil Brenton*, *Lord Dingwall*, *Bangwell*, *Bengwill*, or *Brangwill*, *Bothwell*, etc.

THE STORY is a great favourite, not only in Scandinavian ballads, but also in all northern literature. The magical agency of bed, blankets, sheets, and sword, is elsewhere extended to a chair, a stepping-stone by the bedside (see the *Boy and the Mantle*, First Series, p. 119), or the Billie Blin (see *Young Bekie*, First Series, pp. 6, 7, and *Willie's Lady*, p. 19). The Norwegian tale of Aase and the Prince is known to English readers in Dasent's *Annie the Goosegirl*. The Prince is possessed of a stepping-stone by his bedside, which answers his question night and morning, and enables him to detect the supposititious bride. See also Jamieson's translation of *Ingefred and Gudrunè*, in *Illustrations of Northern Antiquities*, p. 340.

COSPATRICK

1.
   COSPATRICK has sent o'er the faem,
   Cospatrick brought his ladye hame.
2.
   And fourscore ships have come her wi',
   The ladye by the grenewood tree.
3.
   There were twal' and twal' wi' baken bread,
   And twal' and twal' wi' gowd sae reid:
4.
   And twal' and twal' wi' bouted flour,
   And twal' and twal' wi' the paramour.
5.
   Sweet Willy was a widow's son,
   And at her stirrup he did run.
6.
   And she was clad in the finest pall,
   But aye she let the tears down fall.
7.
   'O is your saddle set awrye?
   Or rides your steed for you owre high?

8.
      'Or are you mourning in your tide
      That you suld be Cospatrick's bride?'
9.
      'I am not mourning at this tide
      That I suld be Cospatrick's bride;
10.
      'But I am sorrowing in my mood
      That I suld leave my mother good.
11.
      'But, gentle boy, come tell to me,
      What is the custom of thy countrye?'
12.
      'The custom thereof, my dame,' he says,
      'Will ill a gentle laydye please.
13.
      'Seven king's daughters has our lord wedded,
      And seven king's daughters has our lord bedded;
14.
      'But he's cutted their breasts frae their breast-bane,
      And sent them mourning hame again.
15.
      'Yet, gin you're sure that you're a maid,
      Ye may gae safely to his bed;
16.
      'But gif o' that ye be na sure,
      Then hire some damsell o' your bour.'
17.
      The ladye's call'd her bour-maiden,
      That waiting was into her train.
18.
      18.[1] A mark was two-thirds of a pound.
      'Five thousand merks I will gie thee,
      To sleep this night with my lord for me.'
19.
      When bells were rung, and mass was sayne,
      And a' men unto bed were gane,
20.
      Cospatrick and the bonny maid,
      Into ae chamber they were laid.
21.
      'Now speak to me, blankets, and speak to me, bed,
      And speak, thou sheet, inchanted web;

22.
    'And speak up, my bonny brown sword, that winna lie,
    Is this a true maiden that lies by me?'

23.
    'It is not a maid that you hae wedded,
    But it is a maid that you hae bedded;

24.
    'It is a liel maiden that lies by thee,
    But not the maiden that it should be.'

25.
    O wrathfully he left the bed,
    And wrathfully his claiths on did;

26.
    And he has taen him thro' the ha',
    And on his mother he did ca'.

27.
    'I am the most unhappy man,
    That ever was in Christen land!

28.
    'I courted a maiden, meik and mild,
    And I hae gotten naething but a woman wi' child.'

29.
    'O stay, my son, into this ha',
    And sport ye wi' your merrymen a';

30.
    'And I will to the secret bour,
    To see how it fares wi' your paramour.'

31.
    31.[1] 'stark and sture,' sturdy and strong.
    The carline she was stark and sture,
    She aff the hinges dang the dure.

32.
    'O is your bairn to laird or loun?
    Or is it to your father's groom?'

33.
    'O hear me, mother, on my knee,
    Till my sad story I tell to thee:

34.
    'O we were sisters, sisters seven,
    We were the fairest under heaven.

35.
    'It fell on a summer's afternoon,
    When a' our toilsome task was done,

36.
>   36.¹ 'kavils' = kevels, lots.
>   'We cast the kavils us amang,
>   To see which suld to the grene-wood gang.

37.
>   37.² 'wierd,' fate.
>   'Ohon! alas, for I was youngest,
>   And aye my wierd it was the hardest!

38.
>   'The kavil it on me did fa',
>   Whilk was the cause of a' my woe.

39.
>   'For to the grene-wood I maun gae,
>   To pu' the red rose and the slae;

40.
>   'To pu' the red rose and the thyme,
>   To deck my mother's bour and mine.

41.
>   41.² 'hende' (? = heynde, person).
>   'I hadna pu'd a flower but ane,
>   When by there came a gallant hende,

42.
>   42.¹ 'high-coll'd ... laigh-coll'd,' high-cut ... low-cut.
>   'Wi' high-coll'd hose and laigh-coll'd shoon,
>   And he seem'd to be some king's son.

43.
>   'And be I maid, or be I nae,
>   He kept me there till the close o' day.

44.
>   'And be I maid, or be I nane,
>   He kept me there till the day was done.

45.
>   'He gae me a lock o' his yellow hair,
>   And bade me keep it ever mair.

46.
>   46.¹ 'carknet,' necklace.
>   'He gae me a carknet o' bonny beads,
>   And bade me keep it against my needs.

47.
>   'He gae to me a gay gold ring,
>   And bade me keep it abune a' thing.'

48.
>   'What did ye wi' the tokens rare

49. That ye gat frae that gallant there?'

50. 'O bring that coffer unto me,
And a' the tokens ye sall see.'

51. 'Now stay, daughter, your bour within,
While I gae parley wi' my son.'

52. O she has taen her thro' the ha',
And on her son began to ca':

53. 'What did you wi' the bonny beads,
I bade ye keep against your needs?

54. 'What did you wi' the gay gold ring,
I bade you keep abune a' thing?'

55. 'I gae them to a ladye gay,
I met in grene-wood on a day.

56. 'But I wad gie a' my halls and tours,
I had that ladye within my bours;

57. 'But I wad gie my very life,
I had that ladye to my wife.'

58. 57.² 'burd,' maiden.
'Now keep, my son, your ha's and tours;
Ye have that bright burd in your bours;

59. 'And keep, my son, your very life;
Ye have that ladye to your wife.'

60. Now, or a month was come and gane,
The ladye bore a bonny son;

61. And 'twas weel written on his breast-bane,
'Cospatrick is my father's name.'

61.¹ 'rowe,' roll, wrap.
'O rowe my ladye in satin and silk,
And wash my son in the morning milk.'

YOUNG AKIN

THE TEXT is taken from Buchan's *Ballads of the North of Scotland*, and, like nearly all Buchan's versions, exhibits traces of vulgar remoulding. This ballad in particular has lost much of the original features. Kinloch called his version *Hynde Etin*, Allingham his compilation *Etin the Forester*.

THE STORY is given in a far finer style in romantic Scandinavian ballads. Prior translated two of them, *The Maid and the Dwarf-King*, and *Agnes and the Merman*, both Danish. The Norse ballads on this subject, which may still be heard sung, are exceptionally beautiful. Child says, 'They should make an Englishman's heart wring for his loss.'

In the present version we may with some confidence attribute to Buchan the stanzas from 48 to the end, as well as 15 and 16. The preference is given to Buchan's text merely because it retains features lost in Kinloch's version.

YOUNG AKIN

1.
>LADY Margaret sits in her bower door,
>Sewing at her silken seam;
>She heard a note in Elmond's wood,
>And wish'd she there had been.

2.
>She loot the seam fa' frae her side,
>And the needle to her tae,
>And she is on to Elmond-wood
>As fast as she coud gae.

3.
>She hadna pu'd a nut, a nut,
>Nor broken a branch but ane,
>Till by it came a young hind chiel,
>Says, 'Lady, lat alane.

4.
>4.[4] 'spier,' ask.
>'O why pu' ye the nut, the nut,
>Or why brake ye the tree?
>For I am forester o' this wood:
>Ye shoud spier leave at me.'

5.

  'I'll ask leave at no living man,
   Nor yet will I at thee;
  My father is king o'er a' this realm,
   This wood belongs to me.'

6.
  She hadna pu'd a nut, a nut,
   Nor broken a branch but three,
  Till by it came him Young Akin,
   And gard her lat them be.

7.
  The highest tree in Elmond's wood,
   He's pu'd it by the reet,
  And he has built for her a bower,
   Near by a hallow seat.

8.
  He's built a bower, made it secure
   Wi' carbuncle and stane;
  Tho' travellers were never sae nigh,
   Appearance it had nane.

9.
  He's kept her there in Elmond's wood
   For six lang years and one,
  Till six pretty sons to him she bear,
   And the seventh she's brought home.

10.
  It fell ance upon a day,
   This guid lord went from home,
  And he is to the hunting gane,
   Took wi' him his eldest son.

11.
  And when they were on a guid way,
   Wi' slowly pace did walk,
  The boy's heart being something wae,
   He thus began to talk.

12.
  'A question I woud ask, father,
   Gin ye woudna angry be;'
  'Say on, say on, my bonny boy,
   Ye'se nae be quarrell'd by me.'

13.
  'I see my mither's cheeks aye weet,
   I never can see them dry;
  And I wonder what aileth my mither,

To mourn continually.'

14.

14.⁴ 'stown,' stolen.
'Your mither was a king's daughter,
Sprung frae a high degree,
And she might hae wed some worthy prince
Had she nae been stown by me.

15.

'I was her father's cupbearer,
Just at that fatal time;
I catch'd her on a misty night,
When summer was in prime.

16.

'My luve to her was most sincere,
Her luve was great for me,
But when she hardships doth endure,
Her folly she does see.'

17.

'I'll shoot the buntin' o' the bush,
The linnet o' the tree,
And bring them to my dear mither,
See if she'll merrier be.'

18.

It fell upo' another day,
This guid lord he thought lang,
And he is to the hunting gane,
Took wi' him his dog and gun.

19.

Wi' bow and arrow by his side,
He's aff, single, alane,
And left his seven children to stay
Wi' their mither at hame.

20.

'O I will tell to you, mither,
Gin ye wadna angry be:'
'Speak on, speak on, my little wee boy,
Ye'se nae be quarrell'd by me.'

21.

21.⁴ 'my lane,' by myself. Cp. 26.⁴.
'As we came frae the hynd-hunting,
We heard fine music ring:'
'My blessings on you, my bonny boy,
I wish I'd been there my lane.'

22.
>He's ta'en his mither by the hand,
>His six brithers also,
>And they are on thro' Elmond's wood
>As fast as they coud go.

23.
>23.² 'stratlins,' strayings.
>They wistna weel where they were gaen,
>Wi' the stratlins o' their feet;
>They wistna weel where they were gaen,
>Till at her father's yate.

24.
>'I hae nae money in my pocket,
>But royal rings hae three;
>I'll gie them you, my little young son,
>And ye'll walk there for me.

25.
>'Ye'll gie the first to the proud porter,
>And he will lat you in;
>Ye'll gie the next to the butler-boy,
>And he will show you ben.

26.
>'Ye'll gie the third to the minstrel
>That plays before the King;
>He'll play success to the bonny boy
>Came thro' the wood him lane.'

27.
>He ga'e the first to the proud porter,
>And he open'd an' let him in;
>He ga'e the next to the butler-boy,
>And he has shown him ben;

28.
>He ga'e the third to the minstrel
>That play'd before the King;
>And he play'd success to the bonny boy
>Came thro' the wood him lane.

29.
>Now when he came before the King,
>Fell low down on his knee;
>The King he turned round about,
>And the saut tear blinded his e'e.

30.
>'Win up, win up, my bonny boy,

Gang frae my companie;
Ye look sae like my dear daughter,
My heart will birst in three.'

31.
'If I look like your dear daughter,
A wonder it is none;
If I look like your dear daughter,
I am her eldest son.'

32.
'Will ye tell me, ye little wee boy,
Where may my Margaret be?'
'She's just now standing at your yates,
And my six brithers her wi'.'

33.
'O where are all my porter-boys
That I pay meat and fee,
To open my yates baith wide and braid?
Let her come in to me.'

34.
When she came in before the King,
Fell low down on her knee;
'Win up, win up, my daughter dear,
This day ye'll dine wi' me.'

35.
'Ae bit I canno eat, father,
Nor ae drop can I drink,
Till I see my mither and sister dear,
For lang for them I think!'

36.
When she came before the queen,
Fell low down on her knee;
'Win up, win up, my daughter dear,
This day ye'se dine wi' me.'

37.
'Ae bit I canno eat, mither,
Nor ae drop can I drink,
Until I see my dear sister,
For lang for her I think.'

38.
When that these two sisters met,
She hail'd her courteouslie;
'Come ben, come ben, my sister dear,
This day ye'se dine wi' me.'

39.
>'Ae bit I canno eat, sister,
>Nor ae drop can I drink,
>Until I see my dear husband,
>For lang for him I think.'

40.
>'O where are all my rangers bold
>That I pay meat and fee,
>To search the forest far an' wide,
>And bring Akin to me?'

41.
>Out it speaks the little wee boy:
>'Na, na, this maunna be;
>Without ye grant a free pardon,
>I hope ye'll nae him see!'

42.
>'O here I grant a free pardon,
>Well seal'd by my own han';
>Ye may make search for Young Akin,
>As soon as ever you can.'

43.
>They search'd the country wide and braid,
>The forests far and near,
>And found him into Elmond's wood,
>Tearing his yellow hair.

44.
>44.² 'boun,' go.
>'Win up, win up now, Young Akin,
>Win up and boun wi' me;
>We're messengers come from the court,
>The king wants you to see.'

45.
>'O lat him take frae me my head,
>Or hang me on a tree;
>For since I've lost my dear lady,
>Life's no pleasure to me.'

46.
>'Your head will nae be touch'd, Akin,
>Nor hang'd upon a tree;
>Your lady's in her father's court,
>And all he wants is thee.'

47.
>When he came in before the King,

>   Fell low down on his knee:
>   'Win up, win up now, Young Akin,
>   This day ye'se dine wi' me.'

48.
>   But as they were at dinner set,
>   The boy asked a boun:
>   'I wish we were in the good church,
>   For to get christendoun.

49.
>   'We hae lived in guid green wood
>   This seven years and ane;
>   But a' this time, since e'er I mind,
>   Was never a church within.'

50.
>   'Your asking's nae sae great, my boy,
>   But granted it shall be:
>   This day to guid church ye shall gang,
>   And your mither shall gang you wi'.'

51.
>   When she came unto the guid church,
>   She at the door did stan';
>   She was sae sair sunk down wi' shame,
>   She couldna come farer ben.

52.
>   Then out it speaks the parish priest,
>   And a sweet smile ga'e he:
>   'Come ben, come ben, my lily-flower,
>   Present your babes to me.'

53.
>   Charles, Vincent, Sam and Dick,
>   And likewise James and John;
>   They call'd the eldest Young Akin,
>   Which was his father's name.

54.
>   Then they staid in the royal court,
>   And liv'd wi' mirth and glee,
>   And when her father was deceas'd,
>   Heir of the crown was she.

THE UNQUIET GRAVE

THE TEXT is that communicated to the *Folklore Record* (vol. i. p. 60) by Miss Charlotte Latham, as it was written down from recitation by a girl in Sussex (1868).

THE STORY is so simple, and so reminiscent of other ballads, that we must suppose this version to be but a fragment of some forgotten ballad. Its chief interest lies in the setting forth of a common popular belief, namely, that excessive grief for the dead 'will not let them sleep.' Cp. Tibullus, Lib. 1. Eleg. 1, lines 67, 68:—

> 'Tu Manes ne laede meos: sed parce solutis
>
> Crinibus, et teneris, Delia, parce genis.'

The same belief is recorded in Germany, Scandinavia, India, Persia, and ancient Greece, as well as in England and Scotland (see Sir Walter Scott, *Red-gauntlet*, letter xi., note 2).

There is a version of this ballad beginning—

> 'Proud Boreas makes a hideous noise.'

It is almost needless to add that this is from Buchan's manuscripts.

THE UNQUIET GRAVE

1.
> 'The wind doth blow today, my love,
> And a few small drops of rain;
> I never had but one true love,
> In cold grave she was lain.

2.
> 'I'll do as much for my true love
> As any young man may;
> I'll sit and mourn all at her grave
> For a twelvemonth and a day.'

3.
> The twelvemonth and a day being up,
> The dead began to speak:
> 'Oh who sits weeping on my grave,
> And will not let me sleep?'

4.

'Tis I, my love, sits on your grave,
And will not let you sleep;
For I crave one kiss of your clay-cold lips,
And that is all I seek.'

5.

5.[3,4] Cp. *Clerk Sanders*, 30.[3,4].

'You crave one kiss of my clay-cold lips;
But my breath smells earthy strong;
If you have one kiss of my clay-cold lips,
Your time will not be long.

6.

6.[3] 'ere' = e'er.

''Tis down in yonder garden green,
Love, where we used to walk;
The finest flower that ere was seen
Is withered to a stalk.

7.

'The stalk is withered dry, my love,
So will our hearts decay;
So make yourself content, my love,
Till God calls you away.'

CLERK COLVEN

THE TEXT.—This ballad was one of two transcribed from the now lost Tytler-Brown MS., and the transcript is given here. A considerable portion of the story is lost between stanzas 6 and 7.

THE STORY in its full form is found in a German poem of the twelfth or thirteenth century (*Der Ritter von Stauffenberg*) as well as in many Scandinavian ballads.

In the German tale, the fairy bound the knight to marry no one; on that condition she would come to him whenever he wished, if he were alone, and would bestow endless gifts upon him: if ever he did marry, he would die within three days. Eventually he was forced to marry, and died as he had been warned.

In seventy Scandinavian ballads, the story remains much the same. The hero's name is Oluf or Ole, or some modification of this, of which 'Colvill,' or 'Colven,' as we have it here, is the English equivalent. Oluf, riding out, is accosted by elves or dwarfs, and one of them asks him to dance with her. If he will, a gift is offered; if he will not, a threat is made. Gifts and threats naturally vary in different versions. He attempts to escape, is struck or stabbed fatally, and rides home and dies. His bride is for some time kept in ignorance of his death by various shifts, but at last discovers the truth, and her heart breaks. Oluf's mother dies also.

It will be seen from this account how much is lost in our ballad. But it is evident that Clerk Colven's lady has heard of his previous acquaintance with the mermaiden. This point survives only in four Färöe ballads out of the seventy Scandinavian versions.

The story is also found in French, Breton, Spanish, etc.

CLERK COLVEN

1.
    1.[3] 'gimp,' slender.
    CLARK Colven and his gay ladie,
    As they walked to yon garden green,
    A belt about her middle gimp,
    Which cost Clark Colven crowns fifteen:

2.
    2.[4] 'well-fared may,' well-favoured maiden.

'O hearken weel now, my good lord,
O hearken weel to what I say;
When ye gang to the wall o' Stream,
O gang nae neer the well-fared may.'

3.

'O haud your tongue, my gay ladie,
Tak nae sic care o' me;
For I nae saw a fair woman
I like so well as thee.'

4.

He mounted on his berry-brown steed,
And merry, merry rade he on,
Till he came to the wall o' Stream,
And there he saw the mermaiden.

5.

'Ye wash, ye wash, ye bonny may,
And ay's ye wash your sark o' silk':
'It's a' for you, ye gentle knight,
My skin is whiter than the milk.'

6.

He's ta'en her by the milk-white hand,
He's ta'en her by the sleeve sae green,
And he's forgotten his gay ladie,
And away with the fair maiden.

  * * * * *

7.

7.³ 'leugh,' laughed.
'Ohon, alas!' says Clark Colven,
'And aye sae sair's I mean my head!'
And merrily leugh the mermaiden,
'O win on till you be dead.

8.

8.² 'gare,' strip. See First Series, Introduction, p. 1.
8.³ 'Row,' roll, bind.
'But out ye tak your little pen-knife,
And frae my sark ye shear a gare;
Row that about your lovely head,
And the pain ye'll never feel nae mair.'

9.

Out he has ta'en his little pen-knife,
And frae her sark he's shorn a gare,
Rowed that about his lovely head,
But the pain increased mair and mair.

10.
>10.⁴ 'war,' worse.
>'Ohon, alas!' says Clark Colven,
>'An' aye sae sair's I mean my head!'
>And merrily laugh'd the mermaiden,
>'It will ay be war till ye be dead.'

11.
>11.⁴ 'fleed,' flood.
>Then out he drew his trusty blade,
>And thought wi' it to be her dead,
>But she's become a fish again,
>And merrily sprang into the fleed.

12.
>12.² 'dowy,' sad.
>He's mounted on his berry-brown steed,
>And dowy, dowy rade he home,
>And heavily, heavily lighted down
>When to his ladie's bower-door he came.

13.
>'Oh, mither, mither, mak my bed,
>And, gentle ladie, lay me down;
>Oh, brither, brither, unbend my bow,
>'Twill never be bent by me again.'

14.
>His mither she has made his bed,
>His gentle ladie laid him down,
>His brither he has unbent his bow,
>'Twas never bent by him again.

TAM LIN

ἀλλ' ἦ τοι πρώτιστα λέων γένετ' ἠϋγένειος,

αὐτὰρ ἔπειτα δράκων καὶ πάρδαλις ἠδὲ μέγας σῦς·

γίγνετο δ' ὑγρὸν ὕδωρ καὶ δένδρεον ὑψιπέτηλον.A

Odyssey, IV. 456-8.

THE TEXT here given is from Johnson's *Museum*, communicated by Burns. Scott's version (1802), *The Young Tamlane*, contained certain verses, 'obtained from a gentleman residing near Langholm, which are said to be very ancient, though the language is somewhat of a modern cast.' —'Of a grossly modern invention,' says Child, 'and as unlike popular verse as anything can be.' Here is a specimen:—

'They sing, inspired with love and joy,

Like skylarks in the air;

Of solid sense, or thought that's grave,

You'll find no traces there.'

A copy in the Glenriddell MSS. corresponds very closely with the one here printed, doubtless owing to Burns's friendship with Riddell. Both probably were derived from one common source.

THE STORY.—Although the ballad as it stands is purely Scottish, its main feature, the retransformation of Tam Lin, is found in popular mythology even before Homer's time.

A Cretan ballad, taken down about 1820-30, relates that a young peasant, falling in love with a nereid, was advised by an old woman to seize his beloved by the hair just before cock-crow, and hold her fast, whatever transformation she might undergo. He did so; the nymph became in turn a dog, a snake, a camel, and fire. In spite of all, he retained his hold; and at the next crowing of the cock she regained her beauty, and accompanied him home. After a year, in which she spoke no word, she bore a son. The peasant again applied to the old woman for a cure, and was advised to tell his wife that if she would not speak, he would throw the baby into the oven. On his carrying out the old woman's suggestion the nereid cried out, 'Let go my child, dog!' tore her baby from him, and vanished.

This tale was current among the Cretan peasantry in 1820. Two thousand years before, Apollodorus had told much the same story of Peleus and Thetis (*Bibliotheca*, iii. 13). The chief difference is that it was Thetis who placed her son on the fire, to make him immortal, and Peleus who cried out. *The Tayl of the yong Tamlene* is mentioned in the *Complaint of Scotland* (1549).

Carterhaugh is about a mile from Selkirk, at the confluence of the Ettrick and the Yarrow.

The significance of 34.³, 'Then throw me into well water,' is lost in the present version, by the position of the line *after* the 'burning gleed,' as it seems the reciter regarded the well-water merely as a means of extinguishing the gleed. But the immersion in water has a meaning far deeper and more interesting than that. It is a widespread and ancient belief in folklore that immersion in water (or sometimes milk) is indispensable to the recovery of human shape, after existence in a supernatural shape, or *vice versâ*. The version in the Glenriddell MSS. rightly gives it as the *last* direction to Janet, to be adopted when the transformations are at an end:—

> 'First dip me in a stand o' milk,
>
> And then a stand o' water.'

For the beginning of *Tam Lin*, compare the meeting of Akin and Lady Margaret in Elmond-wood in *Young Akin*.

A.

all' ê toi prôtista leôn genet' êugeneios,

autar epeita drakôn kai pardalis êde megas sus;

gigneto d' hugron hudôr kai dendreon hupsipetêlon.

TAM LIN

1.
> O I forbid you, maidens a',
> That wear gowd on your hair,
> To come or gae by Carterhaugh,
> For young Tam Lin is there.

2.
> 2.² 'wad,' forfeit.
> There's nane that gaes by Carterhaugh
> But they leave him a wad,
> Either their rings, or green mantles,

Or else their maidenhead.

3.

3.⁴ 'bree,' brow.
Janet has kilted her green kirtle
A little aboon her knee,
And she has broded her yellow hair
A little aboon her bree,
And she's awa' to Carterhaugh,
As fast as she can hie.

4.

When she came to Carterhaugh
Tam Lin was at the well,
And there she fand his steed standing,
But away was himsel'.

5.

She had na pu'd a double rose,
A rose but only twa,
Till up then started young Tam Lin,
Says, 'Lady, thou's pu' nae mae.

6.

'Why pu's thou the rose, Janet,
And why breaks thou the wand?
Or why comes thou to Carterhaugh
Withoutten my command?'

7.

'Carterhaugh, it is my ain,
My daddie gave it me;
I'll come and gang by Carterhaugh,
And ask nae leave at thee.'

.   .   .   .   .

8.

8.³ 'snooded,' tied with a fillet.
Janet has kilted her green kirtle
A little aboon her knee,
And she has snooded her yellow hair
A little aboon her bree,
And she is to her father's ha',
As fast as she can hie.

9.

Four and twenty ladies fair
Were playing at the ba',
And out then cam' the fair Janet,
Ance the flower amang them a'.

10.
>　10.⁴ 'glass': perhaps a mistake for 'grass.'
>　Four and twenty ladies fair
>　Were playing at the chess,
>　And out then cam' the fair Janet,
>　As green as onie glass.

11.
>　Out then spak an auld grey knight,
>　Lay o'er the castle wa',
>　And says, 'Alas, fair Janet, for thee
>　But we'll be blamed a'.'

12.
>　'Haud your tongue, ye auld fac'd knight,
>　Some ill death may ye die!
>　Father my bairn on whom I will,
>　I'll father nane on thee.'

13.
>　Out then spak her father dear,
>　And he spak meek and mild;
>　'And ever alas, sweet Janet,' he says,
>　'I think thou gaes wi' child.'

14.
>　'If that I gae wi' child, father,
>　Mysel' maun bear the blame;
>　There's ne'er a laird about your ha'
>　Shall get the bairn's name.

15.
>　'If my love were an earthly knight,
>　As he's an elfin grey,
>　I wadna gie my ain true-love
>　For nae lord that ye hae.

16.
>　'The steed that my true-love rides on
>　Is lighter than the wind;
>　Wi' siller he is shod before,
>　Wi' burning gowd behind.'

17.
>　Janet has kilted her green kirtle
>　A little aboon her knee,
>　And she has snooded her yellow hair
>　A little aboon her bree,
>　And she's awa' to Carterhaugh,
>　As fast as she can hie.

18.
>When she cam' to Carterhaugh,
>Tam Lin was at the well,
>And there she fand his steed standing,
>But away was himsel'.

19.
>She had na pu'd a double rose,
>A rose but only twa,
>Till up then started young Tam Lin,
>Says, 'Lady, thou pu's nae mae.

20.
>'Why pu's thou the rose, Janet,
>Amang the groves sae green,
>And a' to kill the bonie babe
>That we gat us between?'

21.
>'O tell me, tell me, Tam Lin,' she says,
>'For's sake that died on tree,
>If e'er ye was in holy chapel,
>Or christendom did see?'

22.
>'Roxbrugh he was my grandfather,
>Took me with him to bide,
>And ance it fell upon a day
>That wae did me betide.

23.
>23.² 'snell,' keen.
>'And ance it fell upon a day,
>A cauld day and a snell,
>When we were frae the hunting come,
>That frae my horse I fell;
>The Queen o' Fairies she caught me,
>In yon green hill to dwell.

24.
>24.⁴ 'tiend,' tithe.
>'And pleasant is the fairy land,
>But, an eerie tale to tell,
>Ay at the end of seven years
>We pay a tiend to hell;
>I am sae fair and fu' o' flesh,
>I'm fear'd it be mysel'.

25.
>'But the night is Halloween, lady,

> The morn is Hallowday;
> Then win me, win me, an ye will,
> For weel I wat ye may.

26.
> 'Just at the mirk and midnight hour
> The fairy folk will ride,
> And they that wad their true-love win,
> At Miles Cross they maun bide.'

27.
> 'But how shall I thee ken, Tam Lin,
> Or how my true-love know,
> Amang sae mony unco knights
> The like I never saw?'

28.
> 'O first let pass the black, lady,
> And syne let pass the brown,
> But quickly run to the milk-white steed,
> Pu' ye his rider down.

29.
> 'For I'll ride on the milk-white steed,
> And ay nearest the town;
> Because I was an earthly knight
> They gie me that renown.

30.
> 'My right hand will be glov'd, lady,
> My left hand will be bare,
> Cockt up shall my bonnet be,
> And kaim'd down shall my hair;
> And thae's the takens I gie thee,
> Nae doubt I will be there.

31.
> 31.² 'esk,' newt.
> 'They'll turn me in your arms, lady,
> Into an esk and adder;
> But hold me fast, and fear me not,
> I am your bairn's father.

32.
> 'They'll turn me to a bear sae grim,
> And then a lion bold;
> But hold me fast, and fear me not,
> As ye shall love your child.

33.
> 33.² 'gaud,' bar.

'Again they'll turn me in your arms
To a red het gaud of airn;
But hold me fast, and fear me not,
I'll do to you nae harm.

34.

34.² 'gleed,' a glowing coal.
'And last they'll turn me in your arms
Into the burning gleed;
Then throw me into well water,
O throw me in wi' speed.

35.

'And then I'll be your ain true-love,
I'll turn a naked knight;
Then cover me wi' your green mantle,
And cover me out o' sight.'

36.

Gloomy, gloomy was the night,
And eerie was the way,
As fair Jenny in her green mantle
To Miles Cross she did gae.

37.

About the middle o' the night
She heard the bridles ring;
This lady was as glad at that
As any earthly thing.

38.

First she let the black pass by,
And syne she let the brown;
But quickly she ran to the milk-white steed,
And pu'd the rider down.

39.

Sae weel she minded whae he did say,
And young Tarn Lin did win;
Syne cover'd him wi' her green mantle,
As blythe's a bird in spring.

40.

Out then spak the Queen o' Fairies,
Out of a bush o' broom:
'Them that has gotten young Tam Lin
Has gotten a stately groom.'

41.

Out then spak the Queen o' Fairies,
And an angry woman was she:

'Shame betide her ill-far'd face,
And an ill death may she die,
For she's ta'en awa' the bonniest knight
In a' my companie.

42.

42.⁴ 'tree,' wood.

'But had I kend, Tam Lin,' she says,
'What now this night I see,
I wad hae ta'en out thy twa grey een,
And put in twa een o' tree.'

THE CLERK'S TWA SONS O' OWSENFORD, and THE WIFE OF USHER'S WELL

THESE two ballads must be considered together, as the last six verses (18-23) of *The Clerk's Twa Sons*, as here given, are a variant of *The Wife of Usher's Well*.

TEXTS.—*The Clerk's Twa Sons* is taken from Kinloch's MSS., in the handwriting of James Chambers, as it was sung to his grandmother by an old woman.

The Wife of Usher's Well is from Scott's *Minstrelsy of the Scottish Border*, and however incomplete, may well stand alone.

THE STORY has a fairly close parallel in the well-known German ballad, 'Das Schloss in Oesterreich'; and a ballad found both in Spain and Italy has resemblances to each. But in these two ballads, especially in *The Wife of Usher's Well*, the interest lies rather in the impressiveness of the verses than in the story.

THE CLERK'S TWA SONS O' OWSENFORD

1.
    1.[4] 'lair,' lesson. Cp. 16.[1].
    O I will sing to you a sang,
    But oh my heart is sair!
    The clerk's twa sons in Owsenford
    Has to learn some unco lair.

2.
    They hadna been in fair Parish
    A twelvemonth an' a day,
    Till the clerk's twa sons o' Owsenford
    Wi' the mayor's twa daughters lay.

3.
    O word's gaen to the mighty mayor,
    As he sail'd on the sea,
    That the clerk's twa sons o' Owsenford
    Wi' his twa daughters lay.

4.
    'If they hae lain wi' my twa daughters,

>
> Meg and Marjorie,
> The morn, or I taste meat or drink,
> They shall be hangit hie.'

5.
> O word's gaen to the clerk himself,
> As he sat drinkin' wine,
> That his twa sons in fair Parish
> Were bound in prison strong.

6.
> Then up and spak the clerk's ladye,
> And she spak pow'rfully:
> 'O tak with ye a purse of gold,
> Or take with ye three,
> And if ye canna get William,
> Bring Andrew hame to me.'

7.
> 7.[1] etc. 'owsen,' oxen.
> 'O lye ye here for owsen, dear sons,
> Or lie ye here for kye?
> Or what is it that ye lie for,
> Sae sair bound as ye lie?'

8.
> 'We lie not here for owsen, dear father,
> Nor yet lie here for kye;
> But it's for a little o' dear-bought love
> Sae sair bound as we lye.'

9.
> O he's gane to the mighty mayor
> And he spake powerfully:
> 'Will ye grant me my twa sons' lives,
> Either for gold or fee?
> Or will ye be sae gude a man
> As grant them baith to me?'

10.
> 'I'll no' grant ye yere twa sons' lives,
> Neither for gold or fee,
> Nor will I be sae gude a man
> As gie them back to thee;
> Before the morn at twelve o'clock
> Ye'll see them hangit hie.'

11.
> Up and spak his twa daughters,
> And they spak pow'rfully:

'Will ye grant us our twa loves' lives,
Either for gold or fee?
Or will ye be sae gude a man
As grant them baith to me?'

12.
'I 'll no' grant ye yere twa loves' lives,
Neither for gold or fee,
Nor will I be sae gude a man
As grant their lives to thee;
Before the morn at twelve o'clock
Ye'll see them hangit hie.'

13.
O he's ta'en out these proper youths,
And hang'd them on a tree,
And he's bidden the clerk o' Owsenford
Gang hame to his ladie.

14.
His lady sits on yon castle-wa',
Beholding dale and doun,
An' there she saw her ain gude lord
Come walkin' to the toun.

15.
'Ye're welcome, welcome, my ain gude lord,
Ye're welcome hame to me;
But where away are my twa sons?
Ye should hae brought them wi' ye.'

16.
'It's I've putten them to a deeper lair,
An' to a higher schule;
Yere ain twa sons 'ill no' be here
Till the hallow days o' Yule.'

17.
17.² 'dool,' grief.
'O sorrow, sorrow, come mak' my bed,
An' dool come lay me doon!
For I'll neither eat nor drink,
Nor set a fit on ground.'

18.
18 Here begins *The Wife of Usher's Well* in a variant.
The hallow days of Yule are come,
The nights are lang and dark;
An' in an' cam' her ain twa sons,
Wi' their hats made o' the bark.

19.
    'O eat an' drink, my merry men a',
    The better shall ye fare,
    For my twa sons the[y] are come hame
    To me for evermair.'

20.
    20.[3] 'happit,' wrapped.
    She has gaen an' made their bed,
    An' she's made it saft an' fine,
    An' she's happit them wi' her gay mantel,
    Because they were her ain.

21.
    21.[1] 'Linkem,' perhaps a stock ballad-locality, like 'Lin,' etc. See First Series, Introduction, p. 1.
    O the young cock crew i' the merry Linkem,
    An' the wild fowl chirp'd for day;
    The aulder to the younger did say,
    'Dear brother, we maun away.'

22.
    'Lie still, lie still, a little wee while,
    Lie still but if we may;
    For gin my mother miss us away,
    She'll gae mad or it be day.'

23.
    O it's they've ta'en up their mother's mantel,
    And they've hang'd it on the pin:
    'O lang may ye hing, my mother's mantel,
    Or ye hap us again!'

THE WIFE OF USHER'S WELL

1.
    THERE lived a wife at Usher's Well,
    And a wealthy wife was she;
    She had three stout and stalwart sons,
    And sent them o'er the sea.

2.
    2.[3] 'carline,' old woman.
    They hadna been a week from her,
    A week but barely ane,
    When word came to the carline wife
    That her three sons were gane.

3.
>They hadna been a week from her,
>A week but barely three,
>When word came to the carlin wife,
>That her sons she'd never see.

4.
>'I wish the wind may never cease,
>Nor fishes in the flood,
>Till my three sons come hame to me,
>In earthly flesh and blood.'

5.
>5.[4] 'birk,' birch.
>It fell about the Martinmass,
>When nights are lang and mirk,
>The carlin wife's three sons came hame,
>And their hats were o' the birk.

6.
>6.[1] 'syke,' marsh.
>6.[2] 'sheugh,' ditch.
>It neither grew in syke nor ditch,
>Nor yet in ony sheugh;
>But at the gates o' Paradise
>That birk grew fair eneugh.

>. . . . .

7.
>'Blow up the fire, my maidens,
>Bring water from the well;
>For a' my house shall feast this night,
>Since my three sons are well.'

8.
>And she has made to them a bed,
>She's made it large and wide,
>And she's ta'en her mantle her about,
>Sat down at the bedside.

>. . . . .

9.
>Up then crew the red, red cock,
>And up and crew the gray;
>The eldest to the youngest said,
>''Tis time we were away.'

10.
>The cock he hadna craw'd but once,
>And clapp'd his wings at a',

  Whan the youngest to the eldest said,
  'Brother, we must awa'.

11.

  11.² 'channerin',' fretting.
  'The cock doth craw, the day doth daw,
  The channerin' worm doth chide;
  Gin we be mist out o' our place,
  A sair pain we maun bide.

12.

  'Fare-ye-weel, my mother dear!
  Fareweel to barn and byre!
  And fare-ye-weel, the bonny lass
  That kindles my mother's fire!'

  . . . . . .

THE GREAT SILKIE OF SULE SKERRIE

THE TEXT was communicated to the Society of Antiquaries of Scotland by Captain F. W. L. Thomas, who took it down from the dictation of an old woman of Shetland.

THE STORY is concerned with the Finn-myth. The Finns live in the depths of the sea. 'Their transfiguration into seals seems to be more a kind of deception they practise. For the males are described as most daring boatmen, with powerful sweep of the oar, who chase foreign vessels on the sea.... By means of a "skin" which they possess, the men and the women among them are able to change themselves into seals. But on shore, after having taken off the wrappage, they are, and behave like, real human beings.... Many a Finn woman has got into the power of a Shetlander, and borne children to him; but if the Finn woman succeeded in re-obtaining her sea-skin, or seal-skin, she escaped across the water' (Karl Blind in the *Contemporary Review*, September 1881, pp. 399-400). The same writer, in quoting a verse of this ballad, says, 'Shööl Skerry means Seal's Isle.' The whole article is of great interest.

'G. S. L.,' the author of *Shetland Fireside Tales, or the Hermit of Trosswickness* (1877), remarks: 'The belief that witches and wizards came from the coast of Norway disguised as seals was entertained by many of the Shetland peasantry even so late as the beginning of the present century.' He goes on to prove the supernatural character of seals by relating an exploit of his own, in which a gun pointed at a seal refused to go off.

Sule Skerrie is a lonely islet to the north-east of Cape Wrath, about as far therefrom as from the Shetland Isles.

Another version of this ballad, unknown to Child, is given in the Appendix.

THE GREAT SILKIE OF SULE SKERRIE

1.
    1.[1] 'nourris,' nurse, nursing-mother.
    AN eartly nourris sits and sings,
    And aye she sings, 'Ba, lily wean!
    Little ken I my bairnis father,
    Far less the land that he staps in.'

2.
    2.[2] 'grumly,' muddy, dreggy. —JAMIESON.
    Then ane arose at her bed-fit.

An' a grumly guest I'm sure was he:
'Here am I, thy bairnis father,
Although that I be not comelie.

3.

3.² 'silkie,' seal.
'I am a man, upo' the lan',
An' I am a silkie in the sea;
And when I'm far and far frae lan',
My dwelling is in Sule Skerrie.'

4.

4.⁴ 'aught,' have.
'It was na weel,' quo' the maiden fair,
'It was na weel, indeed,' quo' she,
'That the Great Silkie of Sule Skerrie
Suld hae come and aught a bairn to me.'

5.

Now he has ta'en a purse of goud,
And he has pat it upo' her knee,
Sayin', 'Gie to me my little young son,
An' tak thee up thy nourris-fee.

6.

'An' it sall come to pass on a simmer's day,
When the sin shines het on evera stane,
That I will tak my little young son,
An' teach him for to swim the faem.

7.

'An' thu sall marry a proud gunner,
An' a proud gunner I'm sure he'll be,
An' the very first schot that ere he schoots,
He'll schoot baith my young son and me.'

CLERK SANDERS

THE TEXT is given in full from Herd's MSS., where it concludes with a version of *Sweet William's Ghost*; and the last three stanzas, 42-44, are from Scott's later version of the ballad (1833) from recitation. Child divides the ballad as follows:— *Clerk Sanders*, 1-26 of the present version; *Sweet William's Ghost*, 27-41. Scott made 'one or two conjectural emendations in the arrangement of the stanzas.'

THE STORY of this admirable ballad in its various forms is paralleled in one or two of its incidents by a similar collection of Scandinavian ballads. Jamieson introduced into his version certain questions and answers (of the prevaricating type found in a baser form in *Our Goodman*) which are professedly of Scandinavian origin.

CLERK SANDERS

1.
    1.² 'gravel'd green'; probably corrupt: perhaps a green with gravelled walks.
    1.⁴ 'I wat'; cp. 11.², 13.², 15.⁴, etc.
    CLARK Sanders and May Margret
    Walkt ower yon gravel'd green;
    And sad and heavy was the love,
    I wat, it fell this twa between.

2.
    'A bed, a bed,' Clark Sanders said,
    'A bed, a bed, for you and I:'
    'Fye no, fye no,' the lady said,
    'Until the day we married be.

3.
    'For in it will come my seven brothers,
    And a' their torches burning bright;
    They'll say, We hae but ae sister,
    And here her lying wi' a knight.'

4.
    4.² 'gin,' altered in the MS. to 'pin.' In either case, it___part of the door-latch.
    'Ye'l take the sourde fray my scabbord,
    And lowly, lowly lift the gin,
    And you may say, your oth to save,
    You never let Clerk Sanders in.

5.

	'Yele take a napken in your hand,

       'Yele take a napken in your hand,
       And ye'l ty up baith your een,
       An' ye may say, your oth to save,
       That ye saw na Sandy sen late yestreen.

6.

       6.² 'ben,' within.
       'Yele take me in your armes twa,
       Yele carrey me ben into your bed,
       And ye may say, your oth to save,
       In your bower-floor I never tread.'

7.

       She has ta'en the sourde fray his scabbord.
       And lowly, lowly lifted the gin;
       She was to swear, her oth to save,
       She never let Clerk Sanders in.

8.

       She has tain a napkin in her hand,
       And she ty'd up baith her een;
       She was to swear, her oth to save,
       She saw na him sene late yestreen.

9.

       She has ta'en him in her armes twa,
       And carried him ben into her bed;
       She was to swear, her oth to save,
       He never in her bower-floor tread.

10.

       In and came her seven brothers,
       And all their torches burning bright;
       Says thay, We hae but ae sister,
       And see there her lying wi' a knight.

11.

       Out and speaks the first of them,
       'A wat they hay been lovers dear;'
       Out and speaks the next of them,
       'They hay been in love this many a year.'

12.

       12.² 'twain,' separate.
       Out an' speaks the third of them,
       'It wear great sin this twa to twain;'
       Out an' speaks the fourth of them,
       'It wear a sin to kill a sleeping man.'

13.

       Out an' speaks the fifth of them,

'A wat they'll near be twain'd by me;'
Out an' speaks the sixt of them,
'We'l tak our leave an' gae our way.'

14.

Out an' speaks the seventh of them,
'Altho' there wear no a man but me,
I'se bear the brand into my hand
Shall quickly gar Clark Sanders die.'

15.

15 Cp. *The Bonny Birdy*, 15.[1-4] (First Series, p. 28).
15.[2] 'striped,' whetted. See First Series, Introduction, pp. xlix-l.
Out he has ta'en a bright long brand,
And he has striped it throw the straw,
And throw and throw Clarke Sanders' body
A wat he has gard cold iron gae.

16.

16.[3] 'well and wellsom,' probably a corruption of 'wae and waesome,' sad and woful.
Sanders he started, an' Margret she lapt
Intill his arms where she lay;
And well and wellsom was the night,
A wat it was between these twa.

17.

And they lay still, and sleeped sound,
Untill the day began to daw;
And kindly till him she did say,
'It is time, trew-love, ye wear awa'.'

18.

They lay still, and sleeped sound,
Untill the sun began to shine;
She lookt between her and the wa',
And dull and heavy was his een.

19.

She thought it had been a loathsome sweat,
A wat it had fallen this twa between;
But it was the blood of his fair body,
A wat his life days wair na lang.

20.

20.[2] 'thoule,' endure.
'O Sanders, I'le do for your sake
What other ladys would na thoule;
When seven years is come and gone,
There's near a shoe go on my sole.

21.
    'O Sanders, I'le do for your sake
    What other ladies would think mare;
    When seven years is come and gone,
    There's nere a comb go in my hair.

22.

    22.[2] 'lack,' discredit.
    22.[4] 'dowy,' mournful.
    'O Sanders, I'le do for your sake,
    What other ladies would think lack;
    When seven years is come and gone,
    I'le wear nought but dowy black.'

23.
    The bells gaed clinking throw the towne,
    To carry the dead corps to the clay;
    An' sighing says her May Margret,
    'A wat I bide a doulfou' day.'

24.
    In an' come her father dear,
    Stout steping on the floor;
    . . . . .
    . . . . .

25.
    'Hold your toung, my doughter dear,
    Let a' your mourning a-bee;
    I'le carry the dead corps to the clay,
    An' I'le come back an' comfort thee.'

26.
    'Comfort well your seven sons;
    For comforted will I never bee;
    For it was neither lord nor loune
    That was in bower last night wi' mee.'

27.
    Whan bells war rung, an' mass was sung,
    A wat a' man to bed were gone,
    Clark Sanders came to Margret's window,
    With mony a sad sigh and groan.

28.
    'Are ye sleeping, Margret?' he says,
    'Or are ye waking presentlie?
    Give me my faith and trouthe again,
    A wat, trew-love, I gied to thee.'

29.

'Your faith and trouth ye's never get,
Nor our trew love shall never twain,
Till ye come with me in my bower,
And kiss me both cheek and chin.'

30.

30.³,⁴ Cp. *The Unquiet Grave*, 5.³,⁴.
'My mouth it is full cold, Margret,
It has the smell now of the ground;
And if I kiss thy comely mouth,
Thy life days will not be long.

31.

31.¹ 'mid-larf,' probably corrupt: changed by Scott to 'midnight.' The meaning is unknown.
'Cocks are crowing a merry mid-larf,
I wat the wild fule boded day;
Gie me my faith and trouthe again.
And let me fare me on my way.'

32.

'Thy faith and trouth thou shall na get,
And our trew love shall never twin,
Till ye tell me what comes of women
A wat that dy's in strong traveling?'

33.

'Their beds are made in the heavens high,
Down at the foot of our good Lord's knee,
Well set about wi' gillyflowers:
A wat sweet company for to see.

34.

'O, cocks are crowing a merry mid-larf,
A wat the wilde foule boded day;
The salms of Heaven will be sung,
And ere now I'le be misst away.'

35.

35.³ 'shot-window,' a window which opens and shuts. See First Series, Introduction, p. 1.
Up she has tain a bright long wand,
And she has straked her trouth thereon;
She has given [it] him out at the shot-window,
Wi' many a sad sigh and heavy groan.

36.

'I thank you, Margret; I thank you, Margret,
And I thank you heartilie;
Gin ever the dead come for the quick,

Be sure, Margret, I'll come again for thee.'

37.
It's hose an' shoon an' gound alane,
She clame the wall and follow'd him,
Until she came to a green forest,
On this she lost the sight of him.

38.
'Is there any room at your head, Sanders?
Is there any room at your feet?
Or any room at your twa sides,
Whare fain, fain woud I sleep?'

39.
'Thair is na room at my head, Margret,
Thair is na room at my feet;
There is room at my twa sides,
For ladys for to sleep.

40.
40.¹ 'meal,' mould, earth.
'Cold meal is my covering owre,
But an' my winding sheet;
My bed it is full low, I say,
Down among the hongerey worms I sleep.

41.
'Cold meal is my covering owre,
But an' my winding sheet;
The dew it falls na sooner down
Then ay it is full weet.

42.
'But plait a wand o' bonny birk,
And lay it on my breast;
And shed a tear upon my grave,
And wish my saul gude rest.

43.
'And fair Margret, and rare Margret,
And Margret o' veritie,
Gin e'er ye love another man,
Ne'er love him as ye did me.'

44.
Then up and crew the milk-white cock,
And up and crew the grey;
The lover vanish'd in the air,
And she gaed weeping away.

YOUNG HUNTING

THE TEXT is given from two copies in Herd's MSS. as collated by Child, with the exception of two lines, 9.³,⁴, which are taken from a third and shorter copy in Herd's MSS., printed by him in the *Scottish Songs*. Scott's ballad, *Earl Richard*, is described by him as made up from the above-mentioned copies of Herd, with some trivial alterations adopted from tradition—a totally inadequate account of wholesale alterations. Scott also gives a similar ballad in *Lord William*.

THE STORY.—Young Hunting, a king's son, tells a former mistress that he has a new sweetheart whom he loves thrice as well. The lady conceals her anger, plies him with wine, and slays him in his drunken sleep. Her deed unluckily is overseen by a bonny bird, whom she attempts to coax into captivity, but fails. She dresses Young Hunting for riding, and throws him into the Clyde. The king his father asks for him. She swears by corn (see First Series, *Glasgerion*, p. 1) that she has not seen him since yesterday at noon. The king's divers search for him in vain, until the bonny bird reminds them of the method of finding a drowned corpse by the means of candles. The lady still denies her guilt, and accuses her maid 'Catheren,' but the bonfire refuses to consume the innocent Catheren. When the real culprit is put in, she burns like hoky-gren.

The discovery of a drowned body by candles is a recognised piece of folklore. Usually the candle is stuck in a loaf of bread or on a cork, and set afloat in the river; sometimes a hole is cut in a loaf of bread and mercury poured in to weight it; even a chip of wood is used. The superstition still survives. The most rational explanation offered is that as eddies in rapid streams form deep pools, in which a body might easily be caught, so a floating substance indicates the place by being caught in the centre of the eddy.

The failure of the fire to burn an innocent maid is also, of course, a well-known incident.

YOUNG HUNTING

1.
>'O Lady, rock never your young son young
>One hour longer for me,
>For I have a sweetheart in Garlick's Wells
>I love thrice better than thee.

2.
> 'The very sols of my love's feet
> Is whiter then thy face:'
> 'But nevertheless na, Young Hunting,
> Ye'l stay wi' me all night.'

3.
> 3.¹ 'birl'd,' poured; 'him,' *i.e.* for him.
> She has birl'd in him Young Hunting
> The good ale and the beer,
> Till he was as fou drunken
> As any wild-wood steer.

4.
> 4.⁴ See First Series, *Brown Robin*, 7.⁴; *Fause Footrage*, 16.⁴; and Introduction, p. li.
> She has birl'd in him Young Hunting
> The good ale and the wine,
> Till he was as fou drunken
> As any wild-wood swine.

5.
> Up she has tain him Young Hunting,
> And she has had him to her bed,
> .   .   .   .   .
> .   .   .   .   .

6.
> 6.² 'gare,' part of the dress. See First Series, Introduction, p. l.
> And she has minded her on a little penknife,
> That hangs low down by her gare,
> And she has gin him Young Hunting
> A deep wound and a sare.

7.
> Out an' spake the bonny bird,
> That flew abon her head:
> 'Lady, keep well thy green clothing
> Fra that good lord's blood.'

8.
> 8.³ 'flattering,' wagging.
> 'O better I'll keep my green clothing
> Fra that good lord's blood,
> Nor thou can keep thy flattering toung,
> That flatters in thy head.

9.
> 9.⁴ 'wand,' wood, wicker.
> 'Light down, light down, my bonny bird,

    Light down upon my hand,
    And ye sail hae a cage o' the gowd
    Where ye hae but the wand.

10.
    'O siller, O siller shall be thy hire,
    An' goud shall be thy fee,
    An' every month into the year
    Thy cage shall changed be.'

11.
    'I winna light down, I shanna light down,
    I winna light on thy hand;
    For soon, soon wad ye do to me
    As ye done to Young Hunting.'

12.
    She has booted and spir'd him Young Hunting
    As he had been gan to ride,
    A hunting-horn about his neck,
    An' the sharp sourd by his side;
    And she has had him to yon wan water,
    For a' man calls it Clyde.

13.
    13.[1] 'pot,' pot-hole: a hole scooped by the action of the stream in the rock-bed of a river.
    13.[3] 'truff' = turf.
    The deepest pot intill it a'
    She has puten Young Hunting in;
    A green truff upon his breast,
    To hold that good lord down.

14.
    It fell once upon a day
    The king was going to ride,
    And he sent for him Young Hunting,
    To ride on his right side.

15.
    She has turn'd her right and round about,
    She sware now by the corn:
    'I saw na thy son, Young Hunting,
    Sen yesterday at morn.'

16.
    She has turn'd her right and round about,
    She sware now by the moon:
    'I saw na thy son, Young Hunting,
    Sen yesterday at noon.

17.
    17.³ 'duckers,' divers.
    'It fears me sair in Clyde Water
    That he is drown'd therein:'
    O they ha' sent for the king's duckers
    To duck for Young Hunting.

18.
    They ducked in at the tae water-bank,
    They ducked out at the tither:
    'We'll duck no more for Young Hunting
    All tho' he wear our brother.'

19.
    Out an' spake the bonny bird,
    That flew abon their heads:

    .   .   .   .   .
    .   .   .   .   .

20.
    'O he's na drown'd in Clyde Water,
    He is slain and put therein;
    The lady that lives in yon castil
    Slew him and put him in.

21.
    21.³ 'sakeless,' innocent.
    'Leave aff your ducking on the day,
    And duck upon the night;
    Whear ever that sakeless knight lys slain,
    The candels will shine bright.'

22.
    Thay left off their ducking o' the day,
    And ducked upon the night,
    And where that sakeless knight lay slain,
    The candles shone full bright.

23.
    The deepest pot intill it a'
    Thay got Young Hunting in;
    A green turff upon his brest,
    To hold that good lord down.

24.
    24.⁵ 'wyte,' blame.
    24.⁶ 'May,' maid.
    O thay hae sent aff men to the wood
    To hew down baith thorn an' fern,
    That they might get a great bonefire

To burn that lady in.
'Put na the wyte on me,' she says,
'It was her May Catheren.'

25.
Whan thay had tane her May Catheren,
In the bonefire set her in,
It wad na take upon her cheeks,
Nor take upon her chin,
Nor yet upon her yallow hair,
To healle the deadly sin.

26.

26.[6] 'hoky-gren'; 'gren' is a bough or twig; 'hoakie,' according to Jamieson, is a fire that has been covered up with cinders. 'Hoky-gren,' therefore, is perhaps a kind of charcoal. Scott substitutes 'hollin green,' green holly.

Out they hae tain her May Catheren
And they hay put that lady in;
O it took upon her cheek, her cheek,
An' it took upon her chin,
An' it took on her fair body,
She burnt like hoky-gren.

THE THREE RAVENS
and
THE TWA CORBIES

THE TEXTS of these two variations on the same theme are taken from T. Ravenscroft's *Melismata*, 1611, and Scott's *Minstrelsy*, 1803, respectively. There are several other versions of the Scots ballad, while Motherwell prints *The Three Ravens*, changing only the burden.

Chappell (*Popular Music of the Olden Time*) says of the English version that he has been 'favored with a variety of copies of it, written down from memory; and all differing in some respects, both as to words and tune, but with sufficient resemblance to prove a similar origin.' Consciously or not, the ballad, as set by him to its traditional tune, is to be sung without the threefold repetition shown by Ravenscroft, thus compressing two verses of the ballad into each repetition of the tune, and halving the length of the song.

THE THREE RAVENS

1.
>THERE were three rauens sat on a tree,
>*Downe a downe, hay down, hay downe*
>There were three rauens sat on a tree,
>*With a downe*
>There were three rauens sat on a tree,
>They were as blacke as they might be.
>*With a downe derrie, derrie, derrie, downe, downe.*

2.
>The one of them said to his mate,
>'Where shall we our breakefast take?'

3.
>'Downe in yonder greene field,
>There lies a knight slain vnder his shield.

4.
>'His hounds they lie downe at his feete,
>So well they can their master keepe,

5.
>'His haukes they flie so eagerly,
>There's no fowle dare him come nie.'

6.

7.
    Downe there comes a fallow doe,
    As great with yong as she might goe.

8.
    She lift vp his bloudy hed,
    And kist his wounds that were so red.

9.
    She got him vp vpon her backe,
    And carried him to earthen lake.

10.
    9.[1] 'prime,' the first hour of the day.
    She buried him before the prime,
    She was dead her selfe ere euen-song time.

    God send euery gentleman
    Such haukes, such hounds, and such a leman.

THE TWA CORBIES

1.
    AS I was walking all alane,
    I heard twa corbies making a mane,
    The tane unto the t'other say,
    'Where sall we gang and dine to-day?'

2.
    2.[1] 'fail dyke,' turf wall.
    'In behint yon auld fail dyke,
    I wot there lies a new slain knight;
    And nae body kens that he lies there,
    But his hawk, his hound, and lady fair.

3.
    'His hound is to the hunting gane,
    His hawk to fetch the wild-fowl hame,
    His lady's ta'en another mate,
    So we may mak' our dinner sweet.

4.
    4.[1] 'hause-bane,' neck-bone.
    4.[4] 'theek,' thatch.
    'Ye'll sit on his white hause bane,
    And I'll pike out his bonny blue een:
    Wi' ae lock o' his gowden hair,
    We'll theek our nest when it grows bare.

5.

'Mony a one for him makes mane,
But nane sall ken whare he is gane:
O'er his white banes, when they are bare,
The wind sall blaw for evermair.'

YOUNG BENJIE

THE TEXT is given from Scott's *Minstrelsy* (1803). He remarks, 'The ballad is given from tradition.' No. 29 in the Abbotsford MS., 'Scotch Ballads, Materials for Border Minstrelsy,' is *Young Benjie* (or Boonjie as there written) in thirteen stanzas, headed 'From Jean Scott,' and written in William Laidlaw's hand. All of this except the first stanza is transferred, with or without changes, to Scott's ballad, which is nearly twice as long.

THE STORY of this ballad, simple in itself, introduces to us the elaborate question of the 'lyke-wake,' or the practice of watching through the night by the side of a corpse. More about this will be found under *The Lyke-Wake Dirge*, and in the Appendix at the end of this volume. Here it will suffice to quote Sir Walter Scott's introduction:—

'In this ballad the reader will find traces of a singular superstition, not yet altogether discredited in the wilder parts of Scotland. The lykewake, or watching a dead body, in itself a melancholy office, is rendered, in the idea of the assistants, more dismally awful, by the mysterious horrors of superstition. In the interval betwixt death and interment, the disembodied spirit is supposed to hover around its mortal habitation, and, if provoked by certain rites, retains the power of communicating, through its organs, the cause of its dissolution. Such enquiries, however, are always dangerous, and never to be resorted to unless the deceased is suspected to have suffered *foul play*, as it is called.... One of the most potent ceremonies in the charm, for causing the dead body to speak, is setting the door ajar, or half open. On this account, the peasants of Scotland sedulously avoid leaving the door ajar while a corpse lies in the house. The door must either be left wide open or quite shut; but the first is always preferred, on account of the exercise of hospitality usual on such occasions. The attendants must be likewise careful never to leave the corpse for a moment alone, or, if it is left alone, to avoid, with a degree of superstitious horror, the first sight of it.' —(Ed. 1803, vol. iii. pp. 251-2.)

YOUNG BENJIE

1.
   OF a' the maids o' fair Scotland,
   The fairest was Marjorie;
   And young Benjie was her ae true love,
   And a dear true-love was he.

2.

2.⁴ 'plea,' quarrel.
And wow! but they were lovers dear,
And loved fu' constantlie;
But ay the mair when they fell out,
The sairer was their plea.

3.

And they hae quarrelled on a day,
Till Marjorie's heart grew wae,
And she said she'd chuse another luve.
And let young Benjie gae.

4.

And he was stout, and proud hearted,
And thought o't bitterlie,
And he's gaen by the wan moon-light,
To meet his Marjorie.

5.

'O open, open, my true love!
O open, and let me in!'
'I dare na open, young Benjie,
My three brothers are within.

6.

'Ye lied, ye lied, my bonny burd,
Sae loud's I hear ye lie;
As I came by the Lowden banks,
They bade gude e'en to me.

7.

7.³ 'sets,' befits.
'But fare ye weel, my ae fause love,
That I hae loved sae lang!
It sets ye chuse another love,
And let young Benjie gang.'

8.

Then Marjorie turned her round about,
The tear blinding her ee,
'I darena, darena let thee in,
But I'll come down to thee.'

9.

9.⁴ 'linn,' stream.
Then saft she smiled, and said to him,
'O what ill hae I done?'
He took her in his armis twa,
And threw her o'er the linn.

10.

10.³ 'dang,' overcome.
The stream was strang, the maid was stout,
And laith laith to be dang,
But, ere she wan the Lowden banks,
Her fair colour was wan.

11.

Then up bespak her eldest brother,
'O see na ye what I see?'
And out then spak her second brother,
'It's our sister Marjorie!'

12.

Out then spak her eldest brother,
'O how shall we her ken?'
And out then spak her youngest brother,
'There's a honey mark on her chin.'

13.

Then they've ta'en up the comely corpse,
And laid it on the grund:
'O wha has killed our ae sister,
And how can he be found?

14.

'The night it is her low lykewake,
The morn her burial day,
And we maun watch at mirk midnight,
And hear what she will say.'

15.

15.³ 'streikit,' stretched out.
15.⁴ 'wake,' watch.
Wi' doors ajar, and candle-light,
And torches burning clear,
The streikit corpse, till still midnight,
They waked, but naething hear.

16.

16.⁴ 'thraw,' twist.
About the middle o' the night,
The cocks began to craw,
And at the dead hour o' the night,
The corpse began to thraw.

17.

'O wha has done the wrang, sister,
Or dared the deadly sin?
Wha was sae stout, and feared nae dout,
As thraw ye o'er the linn?'

18.
>'Young Benjie was the first ae man,
>I laid my love upon;
>He was sae stout and proud-hearted,
>He threw me o'er the linn.'

19.
>'Sall we young Benjie head, sister,
>Sall we young Benjie hang,
>Or sall we pike out his twa gray een,
>And punish him ere he gang?'

20.
>'Ye mauna Benjie head, brothers,
>Ye mauna Benjie hang,
>But ye maun pike out his twa gray een,
>And punish him ere he gang.

21.
>'Tie a green gravat round his neck,
>And lead him out and in,
>And the best ae servant about your house,
>To wait young Benjie on.

22.

22.⁴ 'scug,' expiate.

>'And ay, at every seven years' end,
>Ye'll tak him to the linn;
>For that's the penance he maun drie,
>To scug his deadly sin.'

THE LYKE-WAKE DIRGE

THE TEXT is given *verbatim et literatim* from John Aubrey's MS. of his *Remains of Gentilisme & Judaisme* (1686-7) in the Lansdowne MSS., No. 231, folio 114 *recto* and *verso*. This text has often been printed before (see Appendix), but always with errors. The only change made here is the placing of Aubrey's marginal notes among the footnotes: the spelling is Aubrey's spelling. The present version was obtained by Aubrey in 1686 from an informant whose father had heard it sung sixty years previously.

Sir Walter Scott's text, better known than Aubrey's, presents very few variations, the chief being 'sleete' for 'fleet' in 1.³ (see below). This would seem to point to the fact that Scott obtained his version from a manuscript, and confused the antique 'ſ' (= s) with 'f.' A collation, incomplete and inexact, of the two texts is given by T. F. Henderson in his edition of the *Minstrelsy* (1902), vol. iii. pp. 170-2.

THE STORY.—This dirge, of course, is not a ballad in the true sense of the word. But it is concerned with myths so widespread and ancient, that as much could be written about the dirge as almost any one of the ballads proper. I have added an Appendix at the end of this volume, to which those interested in the subject may refer. For the present, the following account may suffice.

Ritson found an illustration of this dirge in a manuscript letter, written by one signing himself 'H. Tr.' to Sir Thomas Chaloner, in the Cotton MSS. (Julius, F. vi., fols. 453-462). The date approximately is the end of the sixteenth century (Sir Thomas Chaloner the elder, 1521-1565; the younger, 1561-1615). The letter is concerned with antiquities in Durham and Yorkshire, especially near Guisborough, an estate of the Chaloner family. The sentence referring to the Lyke-Wake Dirge was printed by Scott, to whom it was communicated by Ritson's executor after his death. It is here given as re-transcribed from the manuscript (f. 461 *verso*).

'When any dieth, certaine women singe a songe to the dead body, recytinge the iorney that the partie deceased must goe, and they are of beleife (such is their fondnesse) that once in their liues yt is good to giue a payre of newe shoes to a poore man; forasmuch as after this life they are to pass barefoote through a greate launde full of thornes & furzen, excepte by the meryte of the Almes aforesaid they have redeemed their forfeyte; for at the edge of the launde an aulde man shall meete them with the same shoes that were giuen by the partie when he was liuinge, and after he hath shodde them he dismisseth them to goe through thicke and thin without scratch or scalle.'

The myth of Hell-shoon (Norse, *helsko*) appears under various guises in many folklores. (See Appendix.)

Sir Walter Scott, in printing 'sleete' in 1.³, said: 'The word *sleet*, in the chorus,1 seems to be corrupted from *selt*, or salt; a quantity of which, in compliance with a popular superstition, is frequently placed on the breast of a corpse.' It is true that a superstition to this effect does exist: but 'fleet' is doubtless the right reading. Aubrey glosses it as 'water'; but Murray has shown (*New English Dictionary, s.v.*), by three quotations from wills dated between 1533 and 1570, that 'fire and flet' is an expression meaning simply 'fire and house-room.' 'Flet,' in short, is our modern 'flat' in an unspecialised and uncorrupted form.

[1]. Scott repeats the first stanza at the end of his version.

THE LYKE-WAKE DIRGE

(LANSDOWNE MS., 231, fol. 114 *recto*.)

1.
    1.¹ 'ean,' one.
    1.³ 'Fleet,' water. —*Aubrey's marginal note*. See above.
    THIS ean night, this ean night,
    eve[r]y night and awle:
    Fire and Fleet and Candle-light
    and Christ recieve thy Sawle.

2.
    2.³ Whin is a Furze. —*Aubrey*.
    2.⁴ This line stands in the MS. as here printed.
    When thou from hence doest pass away
    every night and awle
    To Whinny-moor thou comest at last
                    thy silly poor
    and Christ recieve thy ∧ Sawle.

3.
    3.¹ Job cap. xxxi. 19. If I have seen any perish for want of cloathing, or any poor without covering: 20. If his loyns have not blessed me, and if he were not warmed with the fleece of my sheep, &c. —*Aubrey*.
    3.³ There will be hosen and shoon for them. —*Aubrey*.
    If ever thou gave either hosen or shun
    every night and awle
    Sitt thee downe and putt them on
    and Christ recieve thy Sawle.

4.

4.³ 'beane.' The 'a' was inserted by Aubrey after writing 'bene.'
But if hosen nor shoon thou never gave nean
every night &c:
The Whinnes shall prick thee to the bare beane
and Christ recieve thy Sawle.

5.
From Whinny-moor that thou mayst pass
every night &c:
To Brig o' Dread thou comest at last
and Christ &c:
[fol. 114 *verso*]
6.¹ 'no brader than a thread.' Written by Aubrey as here printed over the second half of the line. Probably it indicates a lost stanza. See Appendix.
no brader than a thread.

6.
From Brig of Dread that thou mayst pass
every night &c:
To Purgatory fire thou com'st at last
and Christ &c:

7.
If ever thou gave either Milke or drinke
every night &c:
The fire shall never make thee shrink
and Christ &c:

8.
8.³ 'bane' might be read 'bene.'
But if milk nor drink thou never gave nean
every night &c:
The Fire shall burn thee to the bare bane
and Christ recive thy Sawle.

THE BONNY EARL OF MURRAY

THE TEXT is given from Allan Ramsay's *Tea-Table Miscellany*, where it first appeared in the tenth edition (1740) in vol. iv. pp. 356-7. Child had not seen this, and gave his text from the eleventh edition of 1750. There is, however, scarcely any difference.

THE STORY of the murder of the Earl of Murray by the Earl of Huntly in February 1592 is found in several histories and other accounts:— *The History of the Church of Scotland* (1655) by John Spottiswoode, Archbishop of Glasgow and of St. Andrews: *History of the Western Highlands and Isles of Scotland* (1836) by Donald Gregory: *The History and Life of King James* (the Sixth), ed. T. Thomson, Bannatyne Club, (1825): *Extracts from the Diarey of R[obert] B[irrel], Burges of Edinburgh* (? 1820): and Sir Walter Scott's *Tales of a Grandfather*. The following condensed account may suffice:—James Stewart, son of Sir James Stewart of Doune ('Down,' 6.²), Earl of Murray by his marriage with the heiress of the Regent Murray, 'was a comely personage, of a great stature, and strong of body like a kemp,' whence he was generally known as the Bonny Earl of Murray. In the last months of 1591, a rumour reached the King's ears that the Earl of Murray had assisted in, or at least countenanced, the attack recently made on Holyrood House by Stewart, Earl of Bothwell; and Huntly was commissioned to arrest Murray and bring him to trial. Murray, apprehended at Donibristle (or Dunnibirsel), his mother the Lady Doune's house, refused to surrender to his feudal enemy the Earl of Huntly, and the house was fired. Murray, after remaining behind the rest of his party, rushed out and broke through the enemy, but was subsequently discovered (by the plumes on his headpiece, which had caught fire) and mortally wounded. Tradition says that Huntly was compelled by his followers to incriminate himself in the deed, and struck the dying Murray in the face, whereat the bonny Earl said, 'You have spoiled a better face than your own.'

THE BONNY EARL OF MURRAY

1.
>YE Highlands and ye Lawlands,
>Oh! where have you been?
>They have slain the Earl of Murray,
>And they lay'd him on the green!
>*They have, &c.*

2.

3.
Now wae be to thee, Huntly,
And wherefore did you sae?
I bade you bring him wi' you,
But forbade you him to slay.
I bade, &c.

4.
3.[2] A game of skill and horsemanship.
He was a braw gallant,
And he rid at the ring;
And the bonny Earl of Murray,
Oh! he might have been a King.
And the, &c.

5.
He was a braw gallant,
And he play'd at the ba';
And the bonny Earl of Murray
Was the flower amang them a'.
And the, &c.

6.
5.[2] Probably like the last.
He was a braw gallant,
And he play'd at the glove;
And the bonny Earl of Murray,
Oh! he was the Queen's love.
And the, &c.

6.[3] 'E'er' = ere.
Oh! lang will his lady
Look o'er the castle Down,
E'er she see the Earl of Murray
Come sounding thro' the town.
E'er she, &c.

BONNIE GEORGE CAMPBELL

THE TEXT is from Motherwell's *Minstrelsy*, pp. 44-5.

THE STORY.—Motherwell says it 'is probably a lament for one of the adherents of the house of Argyle, who fell in the battle of Glenlivat, stricken on Thursday, the third day of October, 1594 years.' Another suggestion is that it refers to a Campbell of Calder killed in a feud with Campbell of Ardkinglas, the murder being the result of the same conspiracy which brought the Bonny Earl of Murray to his death. Another version of the ballad, however, gives the name as James, and it is useless and unnecessary to particularise.

BONNIE GEORGE CAMPBELL

1.
>HIE upon Hielands
>And low upon Tay,
>Bonnie George Campbell
>Rade out on a day.
>Saddled and bridled
>And gallant rade he;
>Hame came his gude horse,
>But never cam he!

2.
>2.[4] 'rivin',' tearing.
>2.[7] 'Toom,' empty.
>Out cam his auld mither
>Greeting fu' sair,
>And out cam his bonnie bride
>Rivin' her hair.
>Saddled and bridled
>And booted rade he;
>Toom hame cam the saddle,
>But never cam he!

3.
>3.[3] 'is to big,' remains to be built.
>'My meadow lies green,
>And my corn is unshorn;
>My barn is to big,
>And my babie's unborn.'

Saddled and bridled
And booted rade he;
Toom hame cam the saddle,
But never cam he!

THE LAMENT OF THE BORDER WIDOW

THE TEXT is given from Scott's *Minstrelsy* (1803), vol. iii. pp. 83-4. His introduction states that it was obtained from recitation in the Forest of Ettrick, and that it relates to the execution of a Border freebooter, named Cokburne, by James V., in 1529.

THE STORY referred to above may have once existed in the ballad, but the lyrical dirge as it now stands is obviously corrupted with a broadside-ballad, *The Lady turned Serving-man*, given with 'improvements' by Percy (*Reliques*, 1765, vol. iii. p. 87, etc.). Compare the first three stanzas of the *Lament* with stanzas 3, 4, and 5 of the broadside:—

> 3.
>
> And then my love built me a bower,
>
> Bedeckt with many a fragrant flower;
>
> A braver bower you never did see
>
> Than my true-love did build for me.
>
> 4.
>
> But there came thieves late in the night,
>
> They rob'd my bower, and slew my knight,
>
> And after that my knight was slain,
>
> I could no longer there remain.
>
> 5.
>
> My servants all from me did flye,
>
> In the midst of my extremity,
>
> And left me by my self alone,
>
> With a heart more cold then any stone.

It is of course impossible to compare the bald style of the broadside with the beautiful Scottish dirge; and the difficulty of clothing a bower with lilies, which offends Professor Child, may be disregarded.

THE LAMENT OF THE BORDER WIDOW

1.

1.

MY love he built me a bonny bower,
And clad it a' wi' lilye flour;
A brawer bower ye ne'er did see,
Than my true love he built for me.

2.

There came a man, by middle day,
He spied his sport, and went away;
And brought the king, that very night,
Who brake my bower, and slew my knight.

3.

He slew my knight, to me sae dear;
He slew my knight, and poin'd his gear;
My servants all for life did flee,
And left me in extremitie.

4.

I sew'd his sheet, making my mane;
I watched the corpse, myself alane;
I watched his body, night and day;
No living creature came that way.

5.

I took his body on my back,
And whiles I gaed, and whiles I sate;
I digg'd a grave, and laid him in,
And happ'd him with the sod sae green.

6.

But think na ye my heart was sair,
When I laid the moul' on his yellow hair?
O think na ye my heart was wae,
When I turn'd about, away to gae?

7.

Nae living man I'll love again,
Since that my lovely knight is slain;
Wi' ae lock of his yellow hair,
I'll chain my heart for evermair.

3.² 'poin'd' = poinded, distrained.

BONNY BEE HO'M
and
THE LOWLANDS OF HOLLAND

THE TEXTS are taken respectively from Alexander Fraser Tytler's Brown MS., and from Herd's MSS., vol. i. fol. 49, where it is stated that a verse is wanting.

THE STORY of *Bonny Bee Ho'm* is of the slightest. The gift of the ring and chain occurs in many ballads and folk-tales. For the ring, see *Hind Horn*, 4-6 (First Series, p. 187).

For the lady's vow to put no comb in her hair, occurring in both ballads, compare *Clerk Sanders*, 21.[4]

The Lowlands of Holland is merely a lyrical version of the same theme.

BONNY BEE HO'M

1.
    BY Arthur's Dale as late I went
    I heard a heavy moan;
    I heard a ladie lammenting sair,
    And ay she cried 'Ohone!

2.
    'Ohon, alas! what shall I do,
    Tormented night and day!
    I never loved a love but ane,
    And now he's gone away.

3.
    'But I will do for my true-love
    What ladies woud think sair;
    For seven year shall come and go
    Ere a kaim gang in my hair.

3.
    'There shall neither a shoe gang on my foot,
    Nor a kaim gang in my hair,
    Nor e'er a coal nor candle-light
    Shine in my bower nae mair.'

5.
    She thought her love had been on the sea,

Fast sailling to Bee Ho'm;
But he was in a quiet chamer,
Hearing his ladie's moan.

6.
'Be husht, be husht, my ladie dear,
I pray thee mourn not so;
For I am deep sworn on a book
To Bee Ho'm for to go.'

7.
She has gi'en him a chain of the beaten gowd,
And a ring with a ruby stone:
'As lang as this chain your body binds,
Your blude can never be drawn.

8.
'But gin this ring shoud fade or fail,
Or the stone shoud change its hue,
Be sure your love is dead and gone,
Or she has proved untrue.'

9.
He had no been at Bonny Bee Ho'm
A twelve mouth and a day,
Till, looking on his gay gowd ring,
The stone grew dark and gray.

10.
'O ye take my riches to Bee Ho'm,
And deal them presentlie,
To the young that canna, the auld that maunna,
And the blind that does not see.'

11.
Now death has come into his bower,
And split his heart in twain;
So their twa souls flew up to heaven,
And there shall ever remain.

THE LOWLANDS OF HOLLAND

1.
>   1.⁴ 'twin'd' = twinned, separated.
>   'My love has built a bony ship, and set her on the sea,
>   With seven score good mariners to bear her company;
>   There's three score is sunk, and three score dead at sea,
>   And the Lowlands of Holland has twin'd my love and me.

2.
>   2.³ 'rout,' roar.
>   2.⁴ 'withershins,' backwards, the wrong way, the opposite of the desired way. Often = contrary to the way of the sun, but not necessarily. See note on etymology, Chambers, *Mediæval Stage*, i. 129.
>   'My love he built another ship, and set her on the main,
>   And nane but twenty mariners for to bring her hame;
>   But the weary wind began to rise, and the sea began to rout,
>   My love then and his bonny ship turn'd withershins about.

3.
>   3.¹ 'coif,' cap, head-dress.
>   'There shall neither coif come on my head nor comb come in my hair;
>   There shall neither coal nor candle-light shine in my bower mair;
>   Nor will I love another one until the day I die,
>   For I never lov'd a love but one, and he's drowned in the sea.'

4.
>   4.¹ 'had' = haud, hold.
>   4.² 'neen nae' = need na, need not.
>   'O had your tongue, my daughter dear, be still and be content,
>   There are mair lads in Galloway, ye neen nae sair lament:'
>   'O there is none in Gallow, there's none at a' for me,
>   For I never lov'd a love but one, and he's drowned in the sea.'

FAIR HELEN OF KIRCONNELL

THE TEXT is taken from Scott's *Minstrelsy of the Scottish Border* (1802), vol. i. pp. 72-79, omitting the tedious Part I. Another of many versions may be found in Sir John Sinclair's *Statistical Account of Scotland*, vol. xiii. pp. 275-6, about the year 1794; fourteen stanzas, corresponding to most of Scott's two parts.

THE STORY of the ballad is given in the two above-mentioned books from tradition as follows. Fair Helen, of the clan of Irving or Bell, favoured Adam Fleming (Fleeming) with her love; another suitor, whose name is said to have been Bell, was the choice of the lady's family and friends. The latter lover becoming jealous, concealed himself in the bushes of the banks of the Kirtle, which flows by the kirkyard of Kirconnell, where the true lovers were accustomed to walk. Being discovered lurking there by Helen, he levelled his carbine at Adam Fleming. Helen, however, threw herself into her lover's arms, and received the bullet intended for him: whereupon he slew his rival. He went abroad to Spain and fought against the infidels, but being still inconsolable, returned to Kirconnell, perished on Helen's grave, and was buried beside her. The tombstone, bearing a sword and a cross, with *Hic jacet Adamus Fleming*, is still (says Scott) shown in the churchyard of Kirconnell.

The Flemings were a family belonging to Kirkpatrick-Fleming, a parish in Dumfries which includes Kirconnell.

Wordsworth's version of the story includes the famous rhyme:—

> 'Proud Gordon cannot bear the thoughts
>
> That through his brain are travelling,—
>
> And, starting up, to Bruce's heart
>
> He launch'd a deadly javelin!'

FAIR HELEN OF KIRCONNELL

1.
   I WISH I were where Helen lies,
   Night and day on me she cries,
   O that I were where Helen lies,
   On fair Kirconnell Lee!

2.
   Curst be the heart that thought the thought,
   And curst the hand that fired the shot,
   When in my arms burd Helen dropt,
   And died to succour me.

3.
   O think na ye my heart was sair,
   When my love dropt down and spak nae mair,
   There did she swoon wi' meikle care,
   On fair Kirconnell Lee.

4.
   As I went down the water side,
   None but my foe to be my guide,
   None but my foe to be my guide,
   On fair Kirconnell Lee.

5.
   I lighted down, my sword did draw,
   I hacked him in pieces sma',
   I hacked him in pieces sma',
   For her sake that died for me.

6.
   O Helen fair, beyond compare,
   I'll make a garland of thy hair,
   Shall bind my heart for evermair,
   Untill the day I die.

7.
   O that I were where Helen lies,
   Night and day on me she cries,
   Out of my bed she bids me rise,
   Says, 'Haste, and come to me!'

8.
   O Helen fair! O Helen chaste!
   If I were with thee I were blest,
   Where thou lies low, and takes thy rest
   On fair Kirconnell Lee.

9.

      I wish my grave were growing green,
      A winding-sheet drawn ower my e'en
      And I in Helen's arms lying
      On fair Kirconnell Lee.

10.
      I wish I were where Helen lies,
      Night and day on me she cries,
      And I am weary of the skies,
      For her sake that died for me.

SIR HUGH, OR THE JEW'S DAUGHTER

THE TEXT is given from Jamieson's *Popular Ballads*, as taken down by him from Mrs. Brown's recitation.

THE STORY of the ballad is told at length in at least two ancient monastic records; in the *Annals of the Monastery of Waverley*, the first Cistercian house in England, near Farnham, Surrey (edited by Luard, vol. ii. p. 346, etc., from MS. Cotton Vesp, A. . fol. 150, etc.); more fully in the *Annals of the Monastery at Burton-on-Trent*, Staffordshire (edited by Luard, vol. i. pp. 340, etc., from MS. Cotton Vesp. E. iii. fol. 53, etc.). Both of these give the date as 1255, the latter adding July 31. Matthew Paris also tells the tale as a contemporary event. The details may be condensed as follows.

All the principal Jews in England being collected at the end of July 1255 at Lincoln, Hugh, a schoolboy, while playing with his companions (*jocis ac choreis*) was by them kidnapped, tortured, and finally crucified. His body was then thrown into a stream, but the water, *tantam sui Creatoris injuriam non ferens*, threw the corpse back on to the land. The Jews then buried it; but it was found next morning above-ground. Finally it was thrown into a well, which at once was lit up with so brilliant a light and so sweet an odour, that word went forth of a miracle. Christians came to see, discovered the body floating on the surface, and drew it up. Finding the hands and feet to be pierced, the head ringed with bleeding scratches, and the body otherwise wounded, it was at once clear to all *tanti sceleris auctores detestandos fuisse Judaeos*, eighteen of whom were subsequently hanged.

Other details may be gleaned from various accounts. The name of the Jew into whose house the boy was taken is given as Copin or Jopin. Hugh was eight or nine years old. Matthew Paris adds the circumstance of Hugh's mother (Beatrice by name) seeking and finding him.

The original story has obviously become contaminated with others (such as Chaucer's *Prioresses Tale*) in the course of six hundred and fifty years. But the central theme, the murder of a child by the Jews, is itself of great antiquity; and similar charges are on record in Europe even in the nineteenth century. Further material for the study of this ballad may be found in Francisque Michel's *Hugh de Lincoln* (1839), and J. O. Halliwell [-Phillipps]'s *Ballads and Poems respecting Hugh of Lincoln* (1849).

Percy in the *Reliques* (1765), vol. i. p. 32, says:— 'If we consider, on the one hand, the ignorance and superstition of the times when such stories took their rise, the virulent prejudices of the monks who record them, and the eagerness with which they would be catched up by the barbarous populace as a pretence for plunder; on the other hand, the great danger incurred by the perpetrators, and the inadequate motives they could have to excite them to a crime of so much horror, we may reasonably conclude the whole charge to be groundless and malicious.'

The tune 'as sung by the late Mrs. Sheridan' may be found in John Stafford Smith's *Musica Antiqua* (1812), vol. i. p. 65, and Motherwell's *Minstrelsy*, tune No. 7.

SIR HUGH, OR THE JEW'S DAUGHTER

1.
>FOUR and twenty bonny boys
>Were playing at the ba',
>And by it came him sweet Sir Hugh,
>And he play'd o'er them a'.

2.
>He kick'd the ba' with his right foot,
>And catch'd it wi' his knee,
>And throuch-and-thro' the Jew's window
>He gard the bonny ba' flee.

3.
>He's doen him to the Jew's castell,
>And walk'd it round about;
>And there he saw the Jew's daughter,
>At the window looking out.

4.
>'Throw down the ba', ye Jew's daughter,
>Throw down the ba' to me!'
>'Never a bit,' says the Jew's daughter,
>'Till up to me come ye.'

5.
>'How will I come up? How can I come up?
>How can I come to thee?
>For as ye did to my auld father,
>The same ye'll do to me.'

6.
>She's gane till her father's garden,
>And pu'd an apple red and green;
>'Twas a' to wyle him sweet Sir Hugh,
>And to entice him in.

7.
>She's led him in through ae dark door,

And sae has she thro' nine;
She's laid him on a dressing-table,
And stickit him like a swine.

8.
And first came out the thick, thick blood,
And syne came out the thin,
And syne came out the bonny heart's blood;
There was nae mair within.

9.
She's row'd him in a cake o' lead,
Bade him lie still and sleep;
She's thrown him in Our Lady's draw-well,
Was fifty fathom deep.

10.
When bells were rung, and mass was sung,
And a' the bairns came hame,
When every lady gat hame her son,
The Lady Maisry gat nane.

11.
She's ta'en her mantle her about,
Her coffer by the hand,
And she's gane out to seek her son,
And wander'd o'er the land.

12.
She's doen her to the Jew's castell,
Where a' were fast asleep:
'Gin ye be there, my sweet Sir Hugh,
I pray you to me speak.'

13.
She's doen her to the Jew's garden,
Thought he had been gathering fruit:
'Gin ye be there, my sweet Sir Hugh,
I pray you to me speak.'

14.
She near'd Our Lady's deep draw-well,
Was fifty fathom deep:
'Whare'er ye be, my sweet Sir Hugh,
I pray you to me speak.'

15.
'Gae hame, gae hame, my mither dear.
Prepare my winding sheet,
And at the back o' merry Lincoln
The morn I will you meet.'

16.
>Now Lady Maisry is gane hame,
>Made him a winding sheet,
>And at the back o' merry Lincoln
>The dead corpse did her meet.

17.
>And a' the bells o' merry Lincoln
>Without men's hands were rung,
>And a' the books o' merry Lincoln
>Were read without man's tongue,
>And ne'er was such a burial
>Sin Adam's days begun.

THE DÆMON LOVER

THE TEXT is from Kinloch's MSS., 'from the recitation of T. Kinnear, Stonehaven.' Child remarks of it that 'probably by the fortunate accident of being a fragment' it 'leaves us to put our own construction upon the weird seaman; and, though it retains the homely ship-carpenter, is on the whole the most satisfactory of all the versions.'

THE STORY is told more elaborately in a broadside, and resembles *Enoch Arden* in a certain degree. James Harris, a seaman, plighted to Jane Reynolds, was captured by a press-gang, taken overseas, and, after three years, reported dead and buried in a foreign land. After a respectable interval, a ship-carpenter came to Jane Reynolds, and eventually wedded her, and the loving couple had three pretty children. One night, however, the ship-carpenter being on a three days' journey, a spirit came to the window, and said that his name was James Harris, and that he had come to take her away as his wife. She explains that she is married, and would not have her husband know of this visit for five hundred pounds. James Harris, however, said he had seven ships upon the sea; and when she heard these 'fair tales,' she succumbed, went away with him, and 'was never seen no more.' The ship-carpenter on his return hanged himself.

Scott's ballad in the *Minstrelsy* spoils its own effect by converting the spirit into the devil. An American version of 1858 tells the tale of a 'house-carpenter' and his wife, and alters 'the banks of Italy' to 'the banks of old Tennessee.'

THE DÆMON LOVER

1.
>'O whare hae ye been, my dearest dear,
>These seven lang years and more?'
>'O I am come to seek my former vows,
>That ye promis'd me before.'

2.
>'Awa wi' your former vows,' she says,
>'Or else ye will breed strife;
>Awa wi' your former vows,' she says,
>'For I'm become a wife.

3.
>'I am married to a ship-carpenter,
>A ship-carpenter he's bound;

I wadna he ken'd my mind this nicht
For twice five hundred pound'
*   *   *   *   *

4.

4.⁴ 'begane,' overlaid.
She has put her foot on gude ship-board,
And on ship-board she's gane,
And the veil that hung oure her face
Was a' wi' gowd begane.

5.

She had na sailed a league, a league,
A league but barely twa,
Till she did mind on the husband she left,
And her wee young son alsua.

6.

'O haud your tongue, my dearest dear,
Let all your follies abee;
I'll show whare the white lillies grow,
On the banks of Italie.'

7.

7.⁴ 'gurly,' tempestuous, lowering.
She had na sailed a league, a league,
A league but barely three,
Till grim, grim grew his countenance,
And gurly grew the sea.

8.

'O haud your tongue, my dearest dear,
Let all your follies abee;
I'll show whare the white lillies grow,
In the bottom of the sea.'

9.

He's tane her by the milk-white hand,
And he's thrown her in the main;
And full five-and-twenty hundred ships
Perish'd all on the coast of Spain.

THE BROOMFIELD HILL

THE TEXT is taken from Scott's *Minstrelsy* (1803). It would be of great interest if we could be sure that the reference to 'Hive Hill' in 8.[1] was from genuine Scots tradition. In Wager's comedy *The Longer thou Lived the more Fool thou art* (about 1568) Moros sings a burden:—

'Brome, brome on hill,

The gentle brome on hill, hill,

Brome, brome on Hive hill,

The gentle brome on Hive hill,

The brome stands on Hive hill a.'

Before this date 'Brume, brume on hil' is mentioned in *The Complaynt of Scotlande*, 1549; and a similar song was among Captain Cox's 'ballets and songs, all auncient.'

THE STORY, of a youth challenging a maid, and losing his wager by being laid asleep with witchcraft, is popular and widespread. In the *Gesta Romanorum* is a story of which this theme is one main incident, the other being the well-known forfeit of a pound of flesh, as in the *Merchant of Venice*. Ser Giovanni (*Pecorone*, IV. 1) tells a similar tale, and other variations are found in narrative or ballad form in Iceland, Sweden, Denmark, Italy, and Germany.

Grimm notes the German superstition that the *rosenschwamm* (gall on the wild rose), if laid beneath a man's pillow, causes him to sleep until it be taken away.

THE BROOMFIELD HILL

1.
>THERE was a knight and a lady bright,
>Had a true tryste at the broom;
>The ane gaed early in the morning,
>The other in the afternoon.

2.
>And ay she sat in her mother's bower door,
>And ay she made her mane:
>'O whether should I gang to the Broomfield Hill,
>Or should I stay at hame?

3.
    3.⁴ 'mansworn,' perjured.
    'For if I gang to the Broomfield Hill,
    My maidenhead is gone;
    And if I chance to stay at hame,
    My love will ca' me mansworn.'

4.
    Up then spake a witch-woman,
    Ay from the room aboon:
    'O ye may gang to the Broomfield Hill,
    And yet come maiden hame.

5.
    5.⁴ 'broom-cow,' twig of broom.
    'For when ye gang to the Broomfield Hill,
    Ye'll find your love asleep,
    With a silver belt about his head,
    And a broom-cow at his feet.

6.
    'Take ye the blossom of the broom,
    The blossom it smells sweet,
    And strew it at your true-love's head,
    And likewise at his feet.

7.
    'Take ye the rings off your fingers,
    Put them on his right hand,
    To let him know, when he doth awake,
    His love was at his command.'

8.
    8.² 'hals-bane,' neck-bone. See *The Twa Corbies* (p. 82), 4.¹.
    8.³ 'wittering,' witness.
    She pu'd the broom flower on Hive Hill,
    And strew'd on's white hals-bane,
    And that was to be wittering true
    That maiden she had gane.

9.
    9.² 'coft,' bought.
    'O where were ye, my milk-white steed,
    That I hae coft sae dear,
    That wadna watch and waken me
    When there was maiden here?'

10.
    10.³ 'kin,' kind of. Cp. *Lady Maisry*, 2.² (First Series, p. 70).
    'I stamped wi' my foot, master,

>   And gard my bridle ring,
>   But na kin thing wald waken ye,
>   Till she was past and gane.'

11.
>   'And wae betide ye, my gay goss-hawk,
>   That I did love sae dear,
>   That wadna watch and waken me
>   When there was maiden here.'

12.
>   'I clapped wi' my wings, master,
>   And aye my bells I rang,
>   And aye cry'd, Waken, waken, master,
>   Before the lady gang.'

13.
>   'But haste and haste, my gude white steed.
>   To come the maiden till,
>   Or a' the birds of gude green wood
>   Of your flesh shall have their fill.'

14.
>   14.² 'howm' = holme, the level low ground on the banks of a river or stream. —JAMIESON.
>   'Ye need na burst your gude white steed
>   Wi' racing o'er the howm;
>   Nae bird flies faster through the wood,
>   Than she fled through the broom.'

WILLIE'S FATAL VISIT

THE TEXT is taken from Buchan's *Ballads of the North of Scotland*. It consists largely of familiar fragments. Stanzas 9-11 can be found in *The Grey Cock*.

THE STORY is a trivial piece in Buchan's usual style; but the smiling ghost, which is female (17.[1]), is a delightful novelty. She assumes the position of guardian of Willie's morals, then tears him in pieces, and hangs a piece on every seat in the church, and his head over Meggie's pew!

WILLIE'S FATAL VISIT

1.
 'Twas on an evening fair I went to take the air,
 I heard a maid making her moan;
 Said, 'Saw ye my father? Or saw ye my mother?
 Or saw ye my brother John?
 Or saw ye the lad that I love best,
 And his name it is Sweet William?'

2.
 'I saw not your father, I saw not your mother,
 Nor saw I your brother John;
 But I saw the lad that ye love best,
 And his name it is Sweet William.'

3.
 'O was my love riding? or was he running?
 Or was he walking alone?
 Or says he that he will be here this night?
 O dear, but he tarries long!'

4.
 'Your love was not riding, nor yet was he running,
 But fast was he walking alone;
 He says that he will be here this night to thee,
 And forbids you to think long.'

5.
 Then Willie he has gane to his love's door,
 And gently tirled the pin:
 'O sleep ye, wake ye, my bonny Meggie,
 Ye'll rise, lat your true-love in.'

6.
 6.[1] 'swack,' nimble; 'snack,' quick.

>   The lassie being swack ran to the door fu' snack,
>   And gently she lifted the pin,
>   Then into her arms sae large and sae lang
>   She embraced her bonny love in.

7.
>   'O will ye gang to the cards or the dice,
>   Or to a table o' wine?
>   Or will ye gang to a well-made bed,
>   Well cover'd wi' blankets fine?'

8.
>   'O I winna gang to the cards nor the dice,
>   Nor yet to a table o' wine;
>   But I'll rather gang to a well-made bed,
>   Well-cover'd wi' blankets fine.'

9.
>   'My braw little cock, sits on the house tap,
>   Ye'll craw not till it be day,
>   And your kame shall be o' the gude red gowd,
>   And your wings o' the siller grey.'

10.
>   The cock being fause untrue he was,
>   And he crew an hour ower seen;
>   They thought it was the gude day-light,
>   But it was but the light of the meen.

11.
>   'Ohon, alas!' says bonny Meggie then,
>   'This night we hae sleeped ower lang!'
>   'O what is the matter?' then Willie replied,
>   'The faster then I must gang.'

12.
>   Then Sweet Willie raise, and put on his claise,
>   And drew till him stockings and sheen,
>   And took by his side his berry-brown sword,
>   And ower yon lang hill he's gane.

13.
>   13.⁴ 'fear,' frighten.
>   As he gaed ower yon high, high hill,
>   And down yon dowie den,
>   Great and grievous was the ghost he saw,
>   Would fear ten thousand men.

14.
>   As he gaed in by Mary kirk,
>   And in by Mary stile,

> Wan and weary was the ghost
> Upon sweet Willie did smile.

15.
> 'Aft hae ye travell'd this road, Willie,
> Aft hae ye travell'd in sin;
> Ye ne'er said sae muckle for your saul
> As, My Maker bring me hame!

16.
> 'Aft hae ye travell'd this road, Willie,
> Your bonny love to see;
> But ye'll never travel this road again
> Till ye leave a token wi' me.'

17.
> 17.² 'frae gair to gair,' from side to side.
> 17.⁵ 'dice,' pew.
> Then she has ta'en him Sweet Willie,
> Riven him frae gair to gair,
> And on ilka seat o' Mary's kirk
> O' Willie she hang a share;
> Even abeen his love Meggie's dice,
> Hang's head and yellow hair.

18.
> 18.⁴ 'reave,' tore.
> His father made moan, his mother made moan,
> But Meggie made muckle mair;
> His father made moan, his mother made moan,
> But Meggie reave her yellow hair.

ADAM

THE TEXT of this half-carol, half-ballad is taken from the Sloane MS. 2593, whence we get *Saint Stephen and King Herod* and other charming pieces like the well-known carol, 'I syng of a mayden.' It is written in eight long lines in the MS.

THE STORY.—Wright, who printed the above MS. for the Warton Club in 1856, remarks that Adam was supposed to have remained bound in the *limbus patrum* from the time of his death until the Crucifixion. In the romance of *Owain Miles* (Cotton MS. Calig. A. ii.) the bishops told Owain that Adam was 'yn helle with Lucyfere' for four thousand six hundred and four years. On account of this tradition incorporated in the carol, I have ventured to include it as a ballad, although it does not find a place in Professor Child's collection.

ADAM

1.
    ADAM lay i-bowndyn,
    bowndyn in a bond,
    Fowre thowsand wynter
    thowt he not to long;

2.
    2.⁴ 'here,' their. The 'book' is, of course, the Bible.
    And al was for an appil,
    an appil that he tok,
    As clerkes fyndyn wretyn
    in here book.

3.
    3.⁴ 'hevene' is the old genitive = of heaven.
    Ne hadde the appil take ben,
    the appil taken ben,
    Ne hadde never our lady
    a ben hevene qwen.

4.
    4.³ 'mown' = can or may.
    Blyssid be the tyme
    that appil take was!
    Therfore we mown syngyn
    Deo gracias.

SAINT STEPHEN AND KING HEROD

THE TEXT is taken from the same manuscript as the last. This manuscript is ascribed, from the style of handwriting, to the reign of Henry VI. The ballad is there written without division into stanzas in twenty-four long lines.

THE STORY.—The miraculous resuscitation of a roast fowl (generally a cock, as here), in confirmation of an incredible prophecy, is a tale found in nearly all European countries. Originally, we find, the miracle is connected with the Passion, not the Nativity. See the *Carnal and the Crane*.

An interpolation in a late Greek MS. of the apocryphal Gospel of Nicodemus relates that Judas, having failed to induce the Jews to take back the thirty pieces of silver, went home to hang himself, and found his wife roasting a cock. On his demand for a rope to hang himself, she asked why he intended to do so; and he told her he had betrayed his master Jesus to evil men, who would kill him; yet he would rise again on the third day. His wife was incredulous, and said, 'Sooner shall this cock, roasting over the coals, crow again'; whereat the cock napped his wings and crew thrice. And Judas, confirmed in the truth, straightway made a noose in the rope, and hanged himself.

Thence the miracle-tale spread over Europe. In a Spanish version not only the cock crows, but his partner the hen lays an egg, in asseveration of the truth. The tale is generally connected with the legend of the Pilgrims of St. James; so in French, Spanish, Dutch, Wendish, and Breton ballads.

In 1701 there was printed in London a broadside sheet of carols, headed with a woodcut of the Nativity, by the side of which is printed: 'A religious man, inventing the conceits of both birds and beasts drawn in the picture of our Saviour's birth, doth thus express them:— The cock croweth *Christus natus est*, Christ is born. The raven asked *Quando?* When? The crow replied *Hac nocte*, This night. The ox cryeth out *Ubi? Ubi?* Where? where? The sheep bleated out *Bethlehem*' (Hone's *Every-day Book*).

SAINT STEPHEN AND KING HEROD

1.
>SEYNT Stevene was a clerk
>in kyng Herowdes halle,
>And servyd him of bred and cloth,
>as every kyng befalle.

2.
>
> Stevyn out of kechoun cam
> wyth boris hed on honde,
> He saw a sterre was fayr and brycht
> over Bedlem stonde.

3.
>
> He kyst adoun the bores hed,
> and went in to the halle;
> 'I forsak the, kyng Herowdes,
> and thi werkes alle.

4.
>
> 'I forsak the, kyng Herowdes,
> and thi werkes alle,
> Ther is a chyld in Bedlem born
> is beter than we alle.'

5.
>
> 5.¹ What aileth thee?
> 5.³, etc. 'Lakkyt the,' Dost thou lack.
> 'Quat eylyt the, Stevene?
> quat is the befalle?
> Lakkyt the eyther mete or drynk
> in kyng Herodwes halle?'

6.
>
> 'Lakit me neyther mete ne drynk
> in king Herowdes halle;
> There is a chyld in Bedlem born,
> is beter than we alle.'

7.
>
> 7.¹ 'wod,' mad.
> 7.² 'brede,' rouse, *i.e.* become angry (?).
> 'Quat eylyt the, Stevyn? art thou wod?
> or thou gynnyst to brede?
> Lakkyt the eyther gold or fe,
> or ony ryche wede?'

8.
>
> 'Lakyt me neyther gold ne fe,
> ne non ryche wede;
> Ther is a chyld in Bedlem born,
> schal helpyn us at our nede.'

9.
>
> 'That is al so soth, Stevyn,
> al so soth i-wys,
> As this capoun crowe schal

      that lyth here in myn dysh.'

10.
      That word was not so sone seyd,
      that word in that halle,
      The capoun crew *Cristus natus est!*
      among the lordes alle.

11.
      11.[1], etc. 'Rysyt,' 'ledit,' 'stonit': these are all imperatives.
      11.[2] 'be to,' etc., by twos and all one by one (?). Cp. *Fair Margaret and Sweet William*, 10.[2] (First Series, p. 65).
      'Rysyt up, myn turmentowres,
      be to and al be on,
      And ledit Stevyn out of this town
      and stonit him with ston.'

12.
      Tokyn he Stevene,
      and stonyd hym in the way;
      And therfore is his evyn
      on Crystes owyn day.

THE CHERRY-TREE CAROL

THE TEXT.—As this carol consists of two parts, the first containing the actual story of the cherry-tree, and the second consisting of the angel's song to Joseph, I have taken the first part (stt. 1-12 inclusive) from the version of Sandys (*Christmas Carols*), and the second (stt. 13-17) from W. H. Husk's *Songs of the Nativity*.

THE STORY of the cherry-tree is derived from the Pseudo-Matthew's gospel, and is also to be found in the fifteenth of the Coventry Mysteries. In other languages the fruit chosen is naturally adapted to the country: thus in Provençal it is an apple; elsewhere (as in the original), dates from the palm-tree; and again, a fig-tree.

The second part is often printed as a separate carol, and might well stand alone. Readers of *Westward Ho!* will remember how Amyas Leigh trolls it forth on Christmas Day. Traditional versions are still to be heard in Somerset and Devon.

THE CHERRY-TREE CAROL

1.
>JOSEPH was an old man,
>And an old man was he,
>When he wedded Mary,
>In the land of Galilee.

2.
>Joseph and Mary walked
>Through an orchard good,
>Where was cherries and berries,
>So red as any blood.

3.
>Joseph and Mary walked
>Through an orchard green,
>Where was berries and cherries,
>As thick as might be seen.

4.
>O then bespoke Mary,
>So meek and so mild:
>'Pluck me one cherry, Joseph,
>For I am with child.'

5.

O then bespoke Joseph,
With words most unkind:
'Let him pluck thee a cherry
That got thee with child.'

6.

O then bespoke the babe,
Within his mother's womb:
'Bow down then the tallest tree,
For my mother to have some.'

7.

Then bowed down the highest tree
Unto his mother's hand;
Then she cried, 'See, Joseph,
I have cherries at command.'

8.

O then bespake Joseph:
'I have done Mary wrong;
But cheer up, my dearest,
And be not cast down.'

9.

Then Mary plucked a cherry
As red as the blood;
Then Mary went home
With her heavy load.

10.

Then Mary took her babe,
And sat him on her knee,
Saying, 'My dear son, tell me
What this world will be.'

11.

'O I shall be as dead, mother,
As the stones in the wall;
O the stones in the streets, mother,
Shall mourn for me all.

12.

'Upon Easter-day, mother,
My uprising shall be;
O the sun and the moon, mother,
Shall both rise with me.'

13.

As Joseph was a walking,

He heard an angel sing:
'This night shall be born
Our heavenly king.

14.
'He neither shall be born
In housen nor in hall,
Nor in the place of Paradise,
But in an ox's stall.

15.
'He neither shall be clothed
In purple nor in pall,
But all in fair linen,
As wear babies all.

16.
'He neither shall be rocked
In silver nor in gold,
But in a wooden cradle,
That rocks on the mould.

17.
'He neither shall be christened
In white wine nor red,
But with fair spring water,
With which we were christened.'

THE CARNAL AND THE CRANE

THE TEXT is taken from Sandys' *Christmas Carols*, where it is printed from a broadside. The only alterations, in which I have followed Professor Child, are the obvious correction of 'east' for 'west' (8.^{1}), and the insertion of one word in 16.^{2}, where Child says 'perhaps a preposition has been dropped.'

THE STORY is compounded of popular legends connected with the life and miracles of Christ. For the miracle of the cock, see <u>Saint Stephen and King Herod</u>. The adoration of the beasts is derived from the *Historia de Nativitate Mariæ*, and is repeated in many legends of the infancy of Christ, but is not sufficiently remarkable in itself to be popular in carols. The origin of the miracle of the harvest is unknown, though in a Breton ballad it forms one of the class known as the miracles of the Virgin (cp. *Brown Robyn's Confession*). Swedish, Provençal, Catalan, Wendish, and Belgian folk-tales record similar legends.

It is much to be regretted that this ballad, which from internal evidence (*e.g.* the use of the word 'renne,' 1.^{2}) is to be attributed to an early age, should have become so incoherent and corrupted by oral tradition. No manuscript or printed copy is known earlier than about 1750, when it occurs in broadside form. The very word 'Carnal' has lapsed from the dictionaries, though somewhere it may survive in speech. Stanza 17 is obviously out of place; one may suspect gaps on either side, for surely more beasts than the 'lovely lion' were enumerated, and a new section begins at stanza 18.

THE CARNAL AND THE CRANE

1.
    1.^{2} 'reign' = renne, the old form of run.
    1.^{4} 'Carnal,' jackdaw (? der. *cornicula, corneille*).
    AS I pass'd by a river side,
    And there as I did reign,
    In argument I chanced to hear
    A Carnal and a Crane.

2.
    The Carnal said unto the Crane,
    'If all the world should turn,
    Before we had the Father,
    But now we have the Son!

3.
    'From whence does the Son come,

  From where and from what place?'
  He said, 'In a manger,
  Between an ox and ass.'

4.

  'I pray thee,' said the Carnal,
  'Tell me before thou go,
  Was not the mother of Jesus
  Conceiv'd by the Holy Ghost?'

5.

  'She was the purest virgin,
  And the cleanest from sin;
  She was the handmaid of our Lord,
  And mother of our King.'

6.

  'Where is the golden cradle
  That Christ was rocked in?
  Where are the silken sheets
  That Jesus was wrapt in?'

7.

  'A manger was the cradle
  That Christ was rocked in:
  The provender the asses left
  So sweetly he slept on.'

8.

  There was a star in the east land
  So bright it did appear,
  Into King Herod's chamber,
  And where King Herod were.

9.

  The Wise Men soon espied it,
  And told the king on high
  A princely babe was born that night
  No king could e'er destroy.

10.

  10.[4] 'fences,' times.
  'If this be true,' King Herod said,
  'As thou tellest unto me,
  This roasted cock that lies in the dish
  Shall crow full fences three.'

11.

  The cock soon freshly feather'd was,
  By the work of God's own hand,
  And then three fences crowed he,

      In the dish where he did stand.

12.
      'Rise up, rise up, you merry men all,
      See that you ready be;
      All children under two years old
      Now slain they all shall be.'

13.
      Then Jesus, ah, and Joseph,
      And Mary, that was so pure,
      They travell'd into Egypt,
      As you shall find it sure.

14.
      And when they came to Egypt's land,
      Amongst those fierce wild beasts,
      Mary, she being weary,
      Must needs sit down to rest.

15.
      'Come sit thee down,' says Jesus,
      'Come sit thee down by me,
      And thou shalt see how these wild beasts
      Do come and worship me.'

16.
      First came the lovely lion,
      Which [to] Jesus' grace did spring,
      And of the wild beasts in the field
      The Lion shall be king.

17.
      We'll choose our virtuous princes
      Of birth and high degree,
      In every sundry nation,
      Where'er we come and see.

18.
      Then Jesus, ah, and Joseph,
      And Mary, that was unknown,
      They travelled by a husbandman,
      Just while his seed was sown.

19.
      'God speed thee, man,' said Jesus,
      'Go fetch thy ox and wain,
      And carry home thy corn again
      Which thou this day hast sown.'

20.
      The husbandman fell on his knees

Even upon his face:
'Long time hast thou been looked for,
But now thou art come at last.

21.

21.[4] *i.e.* though all (mankind) be undeserving.
'And I myself do now believe
Thy name is Jesus called;
Redeemer of mankind thou art,
Though undeserving all.'

22.

'The truth, man, thou hast spoken,
Of it thou mayst be sure,
For I must lose my precious blood
For thee and thousands more.

23.

'If any one should come this way,
And enquire for me alone,
Tell them that Jesus passed by
As thou thy seed didst sow.'

24.

After that there came King Herod,
With his train so furiously,
Enquiring of the husbandman
Whether Jesus passed by.

25.

'Why, the truth it must be spoke,
And the truth it must be known;
For Jesus passed by this way
When my seed was sown.

26.

'But now I have it reapen,
And some laid on my wain,
Ready to fetch and carry
Into my barn again.'

27.

'Turn back,' said the captain,
'Your labour and mine's in vain;
It's full three quarters of a year
Since he his seed hath sown.'

28.

So Herod was deceived,
By the work of God's own hand,
And further he proceeded

  Into the Holy Land.

29.
  There's thousands of children young
  Which for his sake did die;
  Do not forbid those little ones,
  And do not them deny.

30.
  The truth now I have spoken,
  And the truth now I have shown;
  Even the Blessed Virgin
  She's now brought forth a son.

DIVES AND LAZARUS

THE TEXT is given from Joshua Sylvester's *A Garland of Christmas Carols*, where it is printed from an old Birmingham broadside.

THE STORY is one which naturally attracted the attention of the popular ballad-maker, and parallel ballads exist in fairly wide European distribution.

Like the *Carnal and the Crane*, the form in which this ballad is now known is no witness of its antiquity. A 'ballet of the Ryche man and poor Lazarus' was licensed to be printed in 1558; 'a ballett, Dyves and Lazarus,' in 1570-1.

In Fletcher's *Monsieur Thomas* (1639), a fiddler says he can sing the merry ballad of *Diverus and Lazarus*. A correspondent in *Notes and Queries* (ser. IV. iii. 76) says he had heard only Diverus, never Dives, and contributes from memory a version as sung by carol-singers at Christmas in Worcestershire, in which the parallelism of the stanzas is pushed so far that, in the lines corresponding to 13.³ and 13.⁴ in the present version, we have the delightfully popular idea—

> 'There is a place prepared in hell,
>
> For to sit upon a serpent's knee.'

Husk (*Songs of the Nativity*) also gives this version, from an eighteenth-century Worcestershire broadside. I have no doubt but that this feature is traditional from the unknown sixteenth-century ballad.

DIVES AND LAZARUS

1.
>   AS it fell out upon a day,
>   Rich Dives he made a feast,
>   And he invited all his friends,
>   And gentry of the best.

2.
>   Then Lazarus laid him down and down,
>   And down at Dives' door:
>   'Some meat, some drink, brother Dives,
>   Bestow upon the poor.'

3.
>   'Thou art none of my brother, Lazarus,
>   That lies begging at my door;
>   No meat nor drink will I give thee,

Nor bestow upon the poor.'

4.
    Then Lazarus laid him down and down,
    And down at Dives' wall:
    'Some meat, some drink, brother Dives,
    Or with hunger starve I shall.'

5.
    'Thou art none of my brother, Lazarus,
    That lies begging at my wall;
    No meat nor drink will I give thee,
    But with hunger starve you shall.'

6.
    Then Lazarus laid him down and down,
    And down at Dives' gate:
    'Some meat, some drink, brother Dives,
    For Jesus Christ his sake.'

7.
    'Thou art none of my brother, Lazarus,
    That lies begging at my gate;
    No meat nor drink will I give thee,
    For Jesus Christ his sake.'

8.
    Then Dives sent out his merry men,
    To whip poor Lazarus away;
    They had no power to strike a stroke,
    But flung their whips away.

9.
    Then Dives sent out his hungry dogs.
    To bite him as he lay;
    They had no power to bite at all,
    But licked his sores away.

10.
    As it fell out upon a day,
    Poor Lazarus sickened and died;
    There came two angels out of heaven.
    His soul therein to guide.

11.
    'Rise up, rise up, brother Lazarus,
    And go along with me;
    For you've a place prepared in heaven,
    To sit on an angel's knee.'

12.
    As it fell out upon a day,

>   Rich Dives sickened and died;
>   There came two serpents out of hell,
>   His soul therein to guide.

13.
>   'Rise up, rise up, brother Dives,
>   And go with us to see
>   A dismal place prepared in hell,
>   From which thou canst not flee.'

14.
>   Then Dives looked up with his eyes.
>   And saw poor Lazarus blest:
>   'Give me one drop of water, brother Lazarus,
>   To quench my flaming thirst.

15.
>   'Oh! had I as many years to abide,
>   As there are blades of grass,
>   Then there would be an end, but now
>   Hell's pains will ne'er be past.

16.
>   'Oh! was I now but alive again,
>   The space of an half hour:
>   Oh! that I'd made my peace secure,
>   Then the devil should have no power.'

BROWN ROBYN'S CONFESSION

THE TEXT is the only one known, that printed by Buchan, *Ballads of the North of Scotland*, and copied into Motherwell's MS.

THE STORY, relating as it does a miracle of the Virgin, is, perhaps, the only one we possess of a class which, in other lands, is so extensive. A similar Scandinavian ballad has a tragical termination, except in one version.

The casting of lots to discover the Jonah of a ship is a feature common to many literatures.

BROWN ROBYN'S CONFESSION

1.
   IT fell upon a Wodensday
   Brown Robyn's men went to sea,
   But they saw neither moon nor sun,
   Nor starlight wi' their ee.

2.
   2.[1] 'kevels,' lots.
   'We'll cast kevels us amang,
   See wha the unhappy man may be;'
   The kevel fell on Brown Robyn,
   The master-man was he.

3.
   'It is nae wonder,' said Brown Robyn,
   'Altho I dinna thrive,
   For wi' my mither I had twa bairns,
   And wi' my sister five.

4.
   'But tie me to a plank o' wude
   And throw me in the sea;
   And if I sink; ye may bid me sink,
   But if I swim, just lat me bee.'

5.
   They've tyed him to a plank o' wude,
   And thrown him in the sea;
   He didna sink, tho' they bade him sink;
   He swim'd, and they bade lat him bee.

6.
   He hadna been into the sea

An hour but barely three,
Till by it came Our Blessed Lady,
Her dear young son her wi'.

7.

'Will ye gang to your men again,
Or will ye gang wi' me?
Will ye gang to the high heavens,
Wi' my dear son and me?'

8.

'I winna gang to my men again,
For they would be feared at mee;
But I woud gang to the high heavens,
Wi' thy dear son and thee.'

9.

'It's for nae honour ye did to me, Brown Robyn,
It's for nae guid ye did to mee;
But a' is for your fair confession
You've made upon the sea.'

JUDAS

THE TEXT is given from a thirteenth-century MS. in the library of Trinity College, Cambridge (B. 14, 39): it is thus the earliest text of any ballad that we possess. In the MS. it is written in long lines, four (or six, as in 4, 12, and 14) to the stanza.

As the language in which it is written is not easily intelligible, I have added a paraphrase on the opposite pages.

THE STORY is of great interest, as it adds to the various legends of Judas a 'swikele' sister. The treachery of Judas has long been popularly explained (from the Gospel of St. John, xii. 3-6) as follows:— Judas, being accustomed as bearer of the bag to take a tithe of all moneys passing through his hands, considered that he had lost thirty pence on the ointment that might have been sold for three hundred pence, and so took his revenge.

A Wendish ballad makes him lose the thirty pieces of silver, intrusted to him for buying bread, in gambling with certain Jews, who, when he had lost everything, suggested that he should sell his Master. Afterwards, in remorse, he rushes away to hang himself. The fir-tree is soft wood and will not bear him. The aspen is hard wood, and will bear him; so he hangs himself on the aspen. Since when, the aspen always trembles in fear of the Judgement day.

JUDAS

HIT wes upon a Scere-thorsday
that ure loverd aros;
Ful milde were the wordes
he spec to Iudas.

1.[1] 'Scere-thorsday,' the Thursday before Easter.

'Iudas, thou most to Iurselem,
oure mete for to bugge;
Thritti platen of selver

PARAPHRASE

IT was upon a Scere-Thursday
That our Lord arose;
Full mild were the words
He spake to Judas.

'Judas, thou must to Jerusalem,
Our meat for to buy;
Thirty plates of silver
Bear thou upon thy back.

thou bere up othi rugge.

'Thou comest fer ithe brode stret,
fer ithe brode strete,
Summe of thine tunesmen
ther thou meist i-mete.'

Imette wid is soster,
the swikele wimon:
'Iudas, thou were wrthe
me stende the wid ston,
For the false prophete
that tou bilevest upon.'

'Be stille, leve soster,
thin herte the to-breke!
Wiste min loverd Crist,
ful wel he wolde be wreke.'

'Iudas, go thou on the roc,
heie up on the ston;
Lei thin heved i my barm,
slep thou the anon.'

6.³ 'barm,' lap, bosom: cp. the romance of *King Horn* (E.E.T.S., 1866), ll. 705-6,

> 'He fond Horn in arme
> On Rymenhilde barme.'

Sone so Iudas
of slepe was awake,
Thritti platen of selver
from hym weren itake.

He drou hym selve bi the cop
that al it lavede ablode:
The Iewes out of Iurselem

2.³ 'plates,' pieces.

'Come thou far in the broad street,
Far in the broad street,
Some of thy townsmen
Where thou might'st meet.'

Being met with his sister,
The treacherous woman:
'Judas, thou wert worthy
One should have stoned thee with stone.
For the false prophet
That thou believest upon.'

'Be still, dear sister,
May thine heart burst thee in twain!
Did my Lord Christ know,
Full well would he be avenged.'

'Judas, go thou on the rock,
High up on the stone;
Lay thine head in my bosom,
Sleep thou anon.'

So soon as Judas
From sleep was awake,
Thirty plates of silver
From him were taken.

He drew himself by the head
So that it all ran with blood,
The Jews out of Jerusalem
Thought he was mad.

- 122 -

awenden he were wode.

8.¹ 'drou,' past tense of *draw*.

Foret hym com the riche Ieu
that heiste Pilatus:
'Wolte sulle thi loverd
that hette Iesus?'

'I nul sulle my loverd
for nones cunnes eiste,
Bote hit be for the thritti platen
that he me bi taiste.'

'Wolte sulle thi lord Crist
for enes cunnes golde?'
'Nay, bote hit be for the platen
that he habben wolde.'

In him com ur lord gon
as is postles seten at mete:
'Wou sitte ye, postles,
ant wi nule ye ete?
Ic am iboust ant isold
today for oure mete.'

12.¹ 'gon' is infinitive; 'cam gon'
= he came on foot, or perhaps at
a foot-pace. This curious
construction is only used with
verbs of motion. Cp. the
Homeric βῆ δ' ἴμεναι.

Up stod him Iudas:
'Lord, am I that [frek]?
I nas never othe stude
ther me the evel spec.'

13.² 'frek,' man: Skeat's
          suggestion.
13.³ 'nas' = ne was.

8.¹ *i.e.* he tore his hair.

Forth to him came the rich Jew,
That hight Pilatus;
'Wilt thou sell thy Lord,
That hight Jesus?'

'I will not sell my Lord
For no kind of goods,
Except it be for the thirty plates
That he entrusted to me.'

'Wilt thou sell thy Lord Christ
For any kind of gold?'
'Nay, except it be for the plates
That he wished to have.'

In came our Lord walking
As his apostles sat at meat:
'How sit ye, apostles,
And why will ye not eat?
I am bought and sold
To-day for our meat.'

Up stood Judas:
'Lord, am I that man?
I was never in the place
Where I spake evil of thee.'

Up stood Peter,

Up him stod Peter,
ant spec wid al is miste:
'Thau Pilatus him come
wid ten hundred cnistes,
Yet Ic wolde, loverd,
for thi love fiste.'

'Still thou be, Peter;
well I the icnowe;
Thou wolt fur sake me thrien
ar the coc him crowe.'

And spoke with all his might:
'Though Pilate should come
With ten hundred knights,
Yet I would, Lord,
For thy love fight.'

'Still be thou, Peter;
Well I thee know;
Thou wilt forsake me thrice
Ere the cock crow.'

THE MAID AND THE PALMER

THE TEXT is from the Percy Folio MS. The only other known text is a fragment from Sir Walter Scott's recollection, printed in C. K. Sharpe's *Ballad Book*.

THE STORY is well known in the folklore of Europe, and is especially common in the Scandinavian languages. As a rule, however, all these ballads blend the story of the woman of Samaria with the traditions concerning Mary Magdalen that were extant in mediæval times.

From the present ballad it could hardly be gathered (except, perhaps, from stanza 11) that the old palmer represents Christ. This point is at once obvious in the Scandinavian and other ballads.

The extraordinary burden in the English ballad is one of the most elaborate in existence, and is quite as inexplicable as any.

The expression 'to lead an ape in hell' (14.[2]) occurs constantly in Elizabethan and later literature, always in connection with women who die, or expect to die, unmarried. Dyce says the expression 'never has been (and *never will be*) satisfactorily explained'; but it was suggested by Steevens that women who had no mate on earth should adopt in hell an ape as a substitute.

THE MAID AND THE PALMER

1.
>THE maid shee went to the well to washe,
>*Lillumwham, Lillumwham*
>The mayd shee went to the well to washe,
>*Whatt then, what then?*
>The maid shee went to the well to washe,
>Dew ffell of her lilly white fleshe.
>*Grandam boy, grandam boy, heye!*
>*Leg a derry Leg a merry mett mer whoope whir*
>*Drivance, Larumben, Grandam boy, heye!*

2.
>2.[1,2] 'White': so in the MS.; perhaps should be 'while' in each case. 'washed' is *washee* in the MS.
>White shee washed & white shee ronge,
>White shee hang'd o' the hazle wand.

3.

There came an old palmer by the way,
Sais, 'God speed thee well, thou faire maid.

4.
'Hast either cupp or can,
To give an old palmer drinke therin?'

5.
Sayes, 'I have neither cupp nor cann,
To give an old palmer drinke therin.'

6.
'But an thy lemman came from Roome,
Cuppes & cannes thou wold ffind soone.'

7.
Shee sware by God & good St. John,
Lemman had shee never none.

8.
Saies, 'Peace, ffaire mayd, you are fforsworne;
Nine children you have borne.

9.
9.¹ 'Three,' Percy's emendation of *They* in the MS.
9.² 'leade,' vat.
'Three were buryed under thy bed's head;
Other three under thy brewing leade;

10.
10.¹ 'yon': MS. *won*.
10.² '&' for *and* =
'Other three on yon play greene;
Count, maide, & there be nine.'

11.
'But I hope you are the good old man
That all the world beleeves upon.

12.
'Old palmer, I pray thee,
Pennaunce that thou wilt give to me.'

13.
'Penance I can give thee none,
But seven yeere to be a stepping-stone.

14.
'Other seaven a clapper in a bell;
Other seven to lead an ape in hell.

15.
'When thou hast thy penance done,
Then thou'st come a mayden home.'

LADY ISABEL AND THE ELF-KNIGHT

THE TEXT is taken from Buchan's *Ballads of the North of Scotland*, where it is entitled *The Gowans sae gay*. This ballad is much better known in another form, *May Colvin (Collin, Collean)*.

THE STORY.—Professor Child says, 'Of all ballads this has perhaps obtained the widest circulation,' and devotes thirty-two pages to its introduction. Known in the south as well as in the north of Europe, the Germans and Scandinavians preserve it in fuller and more ancient forms than the Latin nations.

In the still popular Dutch ballad *Halewijn*, Heer Halewijn sings so sweetly that the king's daughter asks leave to go to him. Her father, mother, and sister remind her that those who have gone to him have never returned; her brother says he does not care where she goes, if she retains her honour. She makes an elaborate toilet, takes the best horse in the king's stables, and joins Halewijn in the wood. They ride till they come to a gallows with many women hanged upon it. Halewijn offers her the choice of the means of her death, because she is fairest of all. She says she will choose the sword, but that Halewijn had better take off his coat, as it would be a pity to splash it with her blood. As he takes it off, she cuts off his head, which, however, continues to talk, suggesting she should blow his horn to warn his friends. She does not fall into this rather obvious trap, nor will she agree to his suggestion that she should rub his neck with a certain ointment. As she rides home, she meets Halewijn's mother, and tells her he is dead. She is received back with great honour and affection in her father's castle.

This is the best form of the story, but many others only a little less full are found in Flanders, Denmark, Sweden, Norway, Iceland, Germany (nearly thirty variants which fall into three main divisions found respectively in North-West, South, and North-East Germany), Poland (where it is extraordinarily common), Bohemia, Servia, France, North Italy, Spain, and Portugal; and a Magyar ballad bears a certain resemblance. On the whole, the English ballad here printed (but not *May Colvin*) and the Danish, Swedish, and Norwegian ballads, would seem to be the best preserved, on account of their retention of the primary notion, that the maid first charms the knight to sleep and then binds him. In *May Colvin* and many of the other European versions, the knight bids her strip off her gown; she asks him to turn away his face as she does so, and when he is not looking, she pushes him into the river or sea.

The remarkable likeness existing between the names of the knight in the many languages, *e.g.* Halewijn (*Dutch*), Ulver, Olmar, Hollemen (*Danish*),

Olbert (*German*), and Elf-knight in English, has caused some speculation as to a common origin. Professor Bugge has gone so far as to conjecture that the whole story is an offshoot of the tale of Judith and Holofernes, the latter name being the originals of the variants given above. While this hypothesis is perhaps too startling to be accepted without further evidence, it must be allowed that there are resemblances in the two stories; and as for the metamorphosis of Holofernes into Halewijn or Olbert, it is at once apparent that such changes are quite within the possibilities of phonetic tradition; and any one who is unwilling to credit this should recollect the Scottish 'keepach' and 'dreeach' (used together or separately), which are derived, almost beyond belief, from 'hypochondriac.'

May Colvin is one of the few ancient ballads still kept in print in broadside form.

LADY ISABEL AND THE ELF-KNIGHT

1.
> FAIR lady Isabel sits in her bower sewing,
> *Aye as the gowans grow gay*
> There she heard an elf-knight blawing his horn.
> *The first morning in May*

2.
> 'If I had yon horn that I hear blawing,
> And yon elf-knight to sleep in my bosom.'

3.
> This maiden had scarcely these words spoken,
> Till in at her window the elf-knight has luppen.

4.
> 'It's a very strange matter, fair maiden,' said he,
> 'I canna blaw my horn but ye call on me.

5.
> 'But will ye go to yon greenwood side?
> If ye canna gang, I will cause you to ride.'

6.
> He leapt on a horse, and she on another,
> And they rode on to the greenwood together.

7.
> 'Light down, light down, Lady Isabel,' said he,
> 'We are come to the place where you are to die.'

8.
> 'Hae mercy, hae mercy, kind sir, on me,
> Till ance my dear father and mother I see.'

9.
>'Seven king's-daughters here hae I slain,
>And ye shall be the eight o' them.'

10.
>'O sit down a while, lay your head on my knee,
>That we may hae some rest before that I die.'

11.
>She stroak'd him sae fast, the nearer he did creep,
>Wi' a sma' charm she lull'd him fast asleep.

12.
>12.[1] 'ban,' bound.
>12.[2] 'dag-durk,' dagger.
>Wi' his ain sword-belt sae fast as she ban him,
>Wi' his ain dag-durk sae sair as she dang him.

13.
>'If seven king's-daughters here ye hae slain,
>Lye ye here, a husband to them a'.'

A NOBLE RIDDLE WISELY EXPOUNDED

THE TEXT is from a broadside of the seventeenth century from the press of Coles, Vere, Wright, and Clarke, now preserved in the Rawlinson collection in the Bodleian Library.

THE STORY of this ballad is one of the common class of riddle-ballads. Some of these riddles are found also in *Captain Wedderburn*.

It is not clear why in 18.[1] 'poyson is greener than the grass.' In *Captain Wedderburn* (17.[1]) it is 'death' that is greener than the grass, which is equally inexplicable. A variant of the latter gives 'virgus' [= verjuice], a kind of vinegar, which obviously means 'green juice.' It is possible that this might come to be regarded as a synonym for 'poyson'; and the next step is to substitute 'death' for 'poyson.'

A NOBLE RIDDLE WISELY EXPOUNDED

1.
>THERE was a lady of the North Country,
>*Lay the bent to the bonny broom*
>And she had lovely daughters three.
>*Fa la la la, fa la la la ra re*

2.
>There was a knight of noble worth
>Which also lived in the North.

3.
>The knight, of courage stout and brave,
>A wife he did desire to have.

4.
>He knocked at the ladie's gate
>One evening when it was late.

5.
>5.[1] The broadsides all give 'youngest' for 'eldest.'
>The eldest sister let him in,
>And pin'd the door with a silver pin.

6.
>The second sister she made his bed,
>And laid soft pillows under his head.

7.
>The youngest daughter that same night,
>She went to bed with this young knight.

8.
>And in the morning, when it was day,
>These words unto him she did say:

9.
>'Now you have had your will,' quoth she,
>'I pray, sir knight, will you marry me?'

10.
>The young brave knight to her replyed,
>'Thy suit, fair maid, shall not be deny'd:

11.
>'If thou canst answer me questions three,
>This very day will I marry thee.'

12.
>'Kind sir, in love, O then,' quoth she,
>'Tell me what your three questions be.'

13.
>'O what is longer than the way,
>Or what is deeper than the sea?

14.
>'Or what is louder than the horn,
>Or what is sharper than a thorn?

15.
>'Or what is greener than the grass,
>Or what is worse than a woman was?'

16.
>'O love is longer than the way,
>And hell is deeper than the sea.

17.
>'And thunder is louder than the horn,
>And hunger is sharper than a thorn.

18.
>'And poyson is greener than the grass,
>And the Devil is worse than woman was.'

19.
>When she these questions answered had,
>The knight became exceeding glad.

20.
>And having truly try'd her wit,
>He much commended her for it.

21.
> And after, as it is verifi'd,
> He made of her his lovely bride.

22.
> So now, fair maidens all, adieu,
> This song I dedicate to you.

23.
> I wish that you may constant prove
> Vnto the man that you do love.

CAPTAIN WEDDERBURN

THE TEXT is from Kinloch's MSS., where it was written down from the recitation of Mary Barr: it is entitled 'The Earl of Rosslyn's Daughter.'

THE STORY is the converse of *A Noble Riddle Wisely Expounded*, in which the maid wins a husband by riddles; in the present one the captain out-riddles the maid. Similar tales are very popular in many lands, being found in Persia, Russia, Norway, Sweden, Denmark, Turkey, Lithuania, East Siberia, etc.

Most of the lady's riddles are found in an old English song, and its traditional derivatives. The song, which is given below, is found in Sloane MS. 2593, which contains other carols and ballads (see pp. 123-8). From this is derived the nursery song beginning—

    'I had four brothers over the sea'

(with many variations:— 'four sisters,' 'six lovers,' 'a true lover'), and with a curious half-Latin refrain which varies between

    Para-mara, dictum, domine,

and

    Peri-meri, dixi, domine.

The following is the song referred to above. It was twice printed by T. Wright from the fifteenth-century MS.

    1.

1.³ 'drowryis' = druries, keepsakes.

I HAVE a yong suster

fer beyondyn the se;

Many be the drowryis

that che sente me.

    2.

2.³ 'dowe,' dove.

Che sente me the cherye,

withoutyn ony ston,

And so che dede [the] dowe,

withoutyn ony bon.

3.

3.¹ 'brere,' brier: here perhaps the 'hip' of the dog-rose (see 7.¹).

3.³ 'lemman,' sweetheart.

Sche sente me the brere,

withoutyn ony rynde,

Sche bad me love my lemman

withoute longgyng.

4.

4.¹ etc. 'xuld' = should.

How xuld ony cherye

be withoute ston?

And how xuld ony dowe

ben withoute bon?

5.

How xuld any brere

ben withoute rynde?

How xuld I love my lemman

without longyng?

6.

Quan the cherye was a flour,

than hadde it non ston;

Quan the dowe was an ey,

than hadde it non bon.

7.

6.³ 'ey,' egg.

7.³ 'hayt that che lovit,' has what she loves.

Quan the brere was onbred,

than hadde it non rynd;

Quan the mayden hayt that che lovit,

che is without longing.

CAPTAIN WEDDERBURN

1.
> THE Lord of Rosslyn's daughter gaed through the wud her lane,
> And there she met Captain Wedderburn, a servant to the king.
> He said unto his livery man, 'Were 't na agen the law,
> I wad tak her to my ain bed, and lay her at the wa'.'

2.
> 2.[4] The 'stock' of a bed is the outer side, and the 'wa" (= wall) the inner.
> Ancient beds were made like boxes with the outer side cut away.
> 'I'm walking here my lane,' she says, 'amang my father's trees;
> And ye may lat me walk my lane, kind sir, now gin ye please.
> The supper-bell it will be rung, and I'll be miss'd awa';
> Sae I'll na lie in your bed, at neither stock nor wa'.'

3.
> He said, 'My pretty lady, I pray lend me your hand,
> And ye'll hae drums and trumpets always at your command;
> And fifty men to guard ye wi', that weel their swords can draw;
> Sae we'll baith lie in ae bed, and ye'll lie at the wa'.'

4.
> 'Haud awa' frae me, kind sir, I pray lat go my hand;
> The supper-bell it will be rung, nae langer maun I stand.
> My father he'll na supper tak, gif I be miss'd awa';
> Sae I'll na lie in your bed, at neither stock nor wa'.'

5.
> 'O my name is Captain Wedderburn, my name I'll ne'er deny,
> And I command ten thousand men, upo' yon mountains high.
> Tho' your father and his men were here, of them I'd stand na awe,
> But should tak ye to my ain bed, and lay ye neist the wa'.'

6.
> Then he lap aff his milk-white steed, and set the lady on,
> And a' the way he walk'd on foot, he held her by the hand;
> He held her by the middle jimp, for fear that she should fa';
> Saying, 'I'll tak ye to my ain bed, and lay thee at the wa'.'

7.
> 7.[1] 'quartering-house,' lodging-house.
> He took her to his quartering-house, his landlady looked ben,
> Saying, 'Monie a pretty ladie in Edinbruch I've seen;
> But sic 'na pretty ladie is not into it a':

Gae, mak for her a fine down-bed, and lay her at the wa'.'

8.
'O haud awa' frae me, kind sir, I pray ye lat me be,
For I'll na lie in your bed till I get dishes three;
Dishes three maun be dress'd for me, gif I should eat them a',
Before I lie in your bed, at either stock or wa'.

9.
9.³ 'gaw,' gall. It is an ancient superstition that the dove or pigeon has no gall, the fact being that the gall-bladder is absent. See Sir Thomas Browne's *Pseudodoxia Epidemica*, iii. 3.

'Tis I maun hae to my supper a chicken without a bane;
And I maun hae to my supper a cherry without a stane;
And I maun hae to my supper a bird without a gaw,
Before I lie in your bed, at either stock or wa'.'

10.
10.³ 'genty,' neat, limber. —JAMIESON.

'Whan the chicken's in the shell, I'm sure it has na bane;
And whan the cherry's in the bloom, I wat it has na stane;
The dove she is a genty bird, she flees without a gaw;
Sae we'll baith lie in ae bed, and ye'll be at the wa'.'

11.
'O haud awa' frae me, kind sir, I pray ye give me owre,
For I'll na lie in your bed, till I get presents four;
Presents four ye maun gie me, and that is twa and twa,
Before I lie in your bed, at either stock or wa'.

12.
'Tis I maun hae some winter fruit that in December grew,
And I maun hae a silk mantil that waft gaed never through;
A sparrow's horn, a priest unborn, this nicht to join us twa,
Before I lie in your bed, at either stock or wa'.'

13.
'My father has some winter fruit that in December grew;
My mither has a silk mantil the waft gaed never through;
A sparrow's horn ye soon may find, there's ane on ev'ry claw,
And twa upo' the gab o' it, and ye shall get them a'.

14.
14.¹ 'yett,' gate.

'The priest he stands without the yett, just ready to come in;
Nae man can say he e'er was born, nae man without he sin;
He was haill cut frae his mither's side, and frae the same let fa':
Sae we'll baith lie in ae bed, and ye'se lie at the wa'.'

15.
'O haud awa' frae me, kind sir, I pray don't me perplex,

  For I'll na lie in your bed till ye answer questions six:
  Questions six ye maun answer me, and that is four and twa,
  Before I lie in your bed, at either stock or wa'.

16.
  'O what is greener than the gress, what's higher than thae trees?
  O what is worse than women's wish, what's deeper than the seas?
  What bird craws first, what tree buds first, what first does on
     them fa'?
  Before I lie in your bed, at either stock or wa'.'

17.
  'Death is greener than the gress, heaven higher than thae trees;
  The devil's waur than women's wish, hell's deeper than the seas;
  The cock craws first, the cedar buds first, dew first on them does fa';
  Sae we'll baith lie in ae bed, and ye'se lie at the wa','

18.
  Little did this lady think, that morning when she raise,
  That this was for to be the last o' a' her maiden days.
  But there's na into the king's realm to be found a blither twa,
  And now she's Mrs. Wedderburn, and she lies at the wa'.

THE ELPHIN KNIGHT

THE TEXT is from a broadside in black letter in the Pepysian Library at Cambridge; bound up at the end of a book published in 1673.

THE STORY of this ballad but poorly represents the complete form of the story as exhibited in many German and other ballads, where alternate bargaining and riddling ensues between a man and a maid. This long series of ballads is akin to the still longer series in which the person upon whom an impossible task is imposed is considered to have got the mastery by retaliating with another impossible task.

The opening stanzas of this ballad correspond closely with those of *Lady Isabel and the Elf-Knight*.

THE ELPHIN KNIGHT

My plaid awa, my plaid awa,
And ore the hill and far awa,
And far awa to Norrowa,
My plaid shall not be blown awa.

1.
THE elphin knight sits on yon hill,
Ba, ba, ba, lilli-ba
He blaws his horn both lowd and shril.
The wind hath blown my plaid awa

2.
He blowes it east, he blowes it west,
He blowes it where he lyketh best.

3.
3.¹ 'kist,' chest.
'I wish that horn were in my kist,
Yea, and the knight in my armes two.'

4.
She had no sooner these words said,
When that the knight came to her bed.

5.
'Thou art over young a maid,' quoth he,
'Married with me thou il wouldst be.'

6.
'I have a sister younger than I,
And she was married yesterday.'

7.
    'Married with me if thou wouldst be,
    A courtesie thou must do to me.

8.
    8.[1] 'sark,' shirt.
    'For thou must shape a sark to me,
    Without any cut or heme,' quoth he.

9.
    'Thou must shape it knife-and-sheerlesse,
    And also sue it needle-threedlesse.'

10.
    'If that piece of courtesie I do to thee,
    Another thou must do to me.

11.
    'I have an aiker of good ley-land,
    Which lyeth low by yon sea-strand.

12.
    12.[1] 'eare,' plough.
    'For thou must eare it with thy horn,
    So thou must sow it with thy corn.

13.
    13.[1] 'bigg,' build.
    'And bigg a cart of stone and lyme,
    Robin Redbreast he must trail it hame.

14.
    'Thou must barn it in a mouse-holl,
    And thrash it into thy shoe's soll.

15.
    15.[1] 'looff,' palm.
    15.[2] 'seek,' sack.
    'And thou must winnow it in thy looff,
    And also seek it in thy glove.

16.
    'For thou must bring it over the sea,
    And thou must bring it dry home to me.

17.
    'When thou hast gotten thy turns well done,
    Then come to me and get thy sark then.'

18.
>'I'll not quite my plaid for my life;
>It haps my seven bairns and my wife.'
>*The wind shall not blow my plaid awa*

19.
>'My maidenhead I'l then keep still,
>Let the elphin knight do what he will.'
>*The wind's not blown my plaid awa*

KING JOHN AND THE ABBOT

THE TEXT here printed is taken from Percy's *Reliques* (1765), vol. ii. p. 302, etc. He compiled his ballad from a broadside and another copy, *Kinge John and Bishoppe*, that he found in his Folio MS.; and since he made it a much more readable ballad than either of his originals, it is reproduced here.

THE STORY.—Riddles asked by a monarch of one of his dependants, and answered by a third person assuming the guise of the person questioned, form the subject of many ancient tales. In Sacchetti's *Novelle* we find both the abbot and his representative, a miller, who answers Bernabò Visconti the four questions, How far is it to heaven? How much water is there in the sea? What is going on in hell? What is the value of my person? The answers to the first two of these are given simply in large numbers and Bernabò told to measure for himself if he does not believe them. The value of Bernabò's person is estimated, as in our ballad, at one piece less than our Lord.

Another favourite question in these ballads is, Where is the centre of the earth? The answer is given by the man planting his staff and saying, 'Here: prove it wrong if you can.'

In the Percy Folio version, the shepherd is the half-brother of the abbot.

KING JOHN AND THE ABBOT OF CANTERBURY

1.
>   AN ancient story Ile tell you anon
>   Of a notable prince, that was called King John;
>   And he ruled England with maine and with might,
>   For he did great wrong, and maintein'd little right.

2.
>   And Ile tell you a story, a story so merrye,
>   Concerning the Abbot of Canterbùrye;
>   How for his house-keeping, and high renowne,
>   They rode post for him to London towne.

3.
>   An hundred men, the king did heare say,
>   The abbot kept in his house every day;
>   And fifty golde chaynes, without any doubt,
>   In velvet coates waited the abbot about.

4.
    'How now, father abbot, I heare it of thee,
    Thou keepest a far better house than mee,
    And for thy house-keeping and high renowne,
    I feare thou work'st treason against my crown.'

5.
    5.[3] 'deere,' harm.
    'My liege,' quo' the abbot, 'I would it were knowne,
    I never spend nothing but what is my owne;
    And I trust, your grace will do me no deere,
    For spending of my owne true-gotten geere.'

6.
    'Yes, yes, father abbot, thy fault it is highe,
    And now for the same thou needest must dye;
    For except thou canst answer me questions three,
    Thy head shall be smitten from thy bodie.

7.
    'And first,' quo' the king, 'when I'm in this stead,
    With my crowne of golde so faire on my head,
    Among all my liege-men so noble of birthe
    Thou must tell me to one penny what I am worthe.

8.
    'Secondlye, tell me, without any doubt,
    How soone I may ride the whole world about;
    And at the third question thou must not shrink,
    But tell me here truly what I do think.'

9.
    'O, these are hard questions for my shallow witt,
    Nor I cannot answer your grace as yet;
    But if you will give me but three weekes space,
    Ile do my endeavour to answer your grace.'

10.
    'Now three weeks space to thee will I give.
    And that is the longest time thou hast to live;
    For if thou dost not answer my questions three,
    Thy lands and thy livings are forfeit to mee.'

11.
    Away rode the abbot all sad at that word,
    And he rode to Cambridge, and Oxenford;
    But never a doctor there was so wise,
    That could with his learning an answer devise.

12.
    Then home rode the abbot of comfort so cold,

        And he mett his shepheard a going to fold:
        'How now, my lord abbot, you are welcome home;
        What newes do you bring us from good king John?'

13.

        'Sad newes, sad newes, shepheard, I must give;
        That I have but three days more to live:
        For if I do not answer him questions three,
        My head will be smitten from my bodìe.

14.

        'The first is to tell him there in that stead,
        With his crowne of golde so fair on his head,
        Among all his liege men so noble of birth,
        To within one penny of what he is worth.

15.

        'The seconde, to tell him, without any doubt,
        How soone he may ride this whole world about:
        And at the third question I must not shrinke,
        But tell him there truly what he does thinke.'

16.

        'Now cheare up, sire abbot, did you never hear yet,
        That a fool he may learn a wise man witt?
        Lend me horse, and serving-men, and your apparel.
        And I'll ride to London to answere your quarrel.

17.

        'Nay frowne not, if it hath been told unto mee,
        I am like your lordship as ever may bee:
        And if you will but lend me your gowne,
        There is none shall knowe us at fair London towne.'

18.

        'Now horses, and serving-men thou shalt have,
        With sumptuous array most gallant and brave;
        With crozier, and miter, and rochet, and cope,
        Fit to appeare 'fore our fader the pope.'

19.

        'Now welcome, sire abbot,' the king he did say,
        ''Tis well thou'rt come back to keepe thy day;
        For an if thou canst answer my questions three,
        Thy life and thy living both saved shall be.

20.

        'And first, when thou seest me here in this stead,
        With my crown of golde so fair on my head,
        Among all my liege-men so noble of birthe,
        Tell me to one penny what I am worth.'

21.
    'For thirty pence our Saviour was sold
    Amonge the false Jewes, as I have bin told;
    And twenty nine is the worth of thee,
    For I thinke, thou art one penny worser than he.'

22.
    22.[1] 'Meaning probably St. Botolph.' —*Percy's note*. But the Folio gives St. Andrew, so that it is Percy's own emendation.
    The king he laughed, and swore by St. Bittel,
    'I did not think I had been worth so littel!
    —Now secondly tell me, without any doubt,
    How soone I may ride this whole world about.'

23.
    'You must rise with the sun, and ride with the same,
    Until the next morning he riseth againe;
    And then your grace need not make any doubt,
    But in twenty-four hours you'll ride it about.'

24.
    The king he laughed, and swore by St. Jone,
    'I did not think it could be gone so soone!
    —Now from the third question thou must not shrinke,
    But tell me here truly what I do thinke.'

25.
    'Yea, that I shall do, and make your grace merry:
    You thinke I'm the abbot of Canterbùrye;
    But I'm his poor shepheard, as plain you may see,
    That am come to beg pardon for him and for me.'

26.
    The king he laughed, and swore by the masse,
    'Ile make thee lord abbot this day in his place!'
    'Now naye, my liege, be not in such speede,
    For alacke I can neither write, ne reade.'

27.
    'Four nobles a weeke, then I will give thee,
    For this merry jest thou hast showne unto mee;
    And tell the old abbot when thou comest home,
    Thou hast brought him a pardon from good king John.'

THE FAUSE KNIGHT UPON THE ROAD

THE TEXT is taken from the Introduction to Motherwell's *Minstrelsy*, p. lxxiv.

THE STORY appears to be a conversation between a wee boy and the devil, the latter under the guise of a knight. The boy will be carried off unless he can 'have the last word,' a charm of great power against all evil spirits.

A very similar ballad, of repartees between an old crone and a wee boy, was found at the Lappfiord, Finland.

THE FAUSE KNIGHT UPON THE ROAD

1.
    'O whare are ye gaun?'
    Quo the fause knicht upon the road:
    'I'm gaun to the scule,'
    Quo' the wee boy, and still he stude.

2.
    2.² 'Atweel,' = I wot well, truly.
    'What is that upon your back?'
    'Atweel it is my bukes.'

3.
    3.² 'peit,' peat, carried to school to contribute to the fire.
    'What's that ye've got in your arm?'
    'Atweel it is my peit.'

4.
    4.¹ 'Wha's aucht,' who owns.
    'Wha's aucht they sheep?'
    'They're mine and my mither's.'

5.
    'How monie o' them are mine?'
    'A' they that hae blue tails.'

6.
    'I wiss ye were on yon tree:'
    'And a gude ladder under me.'

7.
    'And the ladder for to break:'
    'And you for to fa' down.'

8.
>   'I wiss ye were in yon sie:'
>   'And a gude bottom under me.'

9.
>   'And the bottom for to break:'
>   'And ye to be drowned.'

THE LORD OF LEARNE

THE TEXT is from the Percy Folio MS., with the spelling modernised, except in two or three instances for the sake of the rhyme (13.⁴) or metre (102.²). Other alterations, as suggested by Child, are noted. Apart from the irregularities of metre, this ballad is remarkable for the large proportion of 'e' rhymes, which are found in 71 stanzas, or two-thirds of the whole. The redundant 'that,' which is a feature of the Percy Folio, also occurs frequently—in eleven places, three of which are in optative sentences (8.², 14.⁴, 91.⁴).

The ballad is more commonly known as *The Lord of Lorne*, under which title we find it registered in the Stationers' Company on October 6, 1580. Guilpin refers to it in his *Skialethia* (1598), Satire 1, ll. 107-108:—

'... the old ballad of the Lord of Lorne

Whose last line in King Harry's day was born.'

Probably this implies little more than that the ballad was known in Henry VIII.'s day. Three broadsides are known, two in the Roxburghe and one in the Pepys collection. Both the Roxburghe ballads are later than the Folio version.

THE STORY is derived from that of *Roswall and Lillian*. Roswall, the king's son, of Naples, overhearing three lords bewailing their long imprisonment, promised to set them free, and did so by stealing the keys from under the king's pillow at night. The king, on hearing of their escape, vowed to slay at sight the man who had set them free. The queen, however, interceding for her son, Roswall was banished under charge of a steward. From this point our ballad follows the romance fairly closely. Roswall and the steward, after changing places, entered the kingdom of Bealm. At length Roswall, under the name Dissawar (see 29.², etc.), became chamberlain to the Princess Lillian, and she fell in love with him. The King of Bealm meanwhile sent to the King of Naples, proposing to wed his daughter to the young prince of Naples, and the Neapolitan king assented. A joust was proclaimed, and Lillian told Dissawar to joust for her, but he preferred to go a-hunting. However, in the wood he found the three knights he had helped to escape, and they equipped him for the three days' tourney, in which he defeated the steward. He did not, however, proclaim himself, and Lillian was forced to ask the king herself for Dissawar; but her father married her to the steward. During the wedding feast the three Neapolitan lords appeared, but would not acknowledge the steward as their prince, and went in search of Roswall, who told the king of the steward's treachery, and announced himself to be the victor of the jousts. The steward was hanged and Roswall married to Lillian.

Other romances and stories exist, with similar foundations, especially amongst the Slavic nations. But the best known is the *Goose-girl* (*Die Gänsemagd*) of the Grimms, where the sexes are reversed. A connection may be traced between the horse Falada's head and the gelding of the ballad; and the trick of a person, who is sworn to secrecy, divulging the secret to some object (as the gelding, here; but more often a stove or oven) in the presence of witnesses has obtained a wide vogue.

THE LORD OF LEARNE

1.
>IT was the worthy lord of Learne,
>He was a lord of a high degree;
>He had no more children but one son,
>He set him to school to learn courtesy.

2.
>Learning did so proceed with that child—
>I tell you all in verity—
>He learned more upon one day
>Than other children did on three.

3.
>And then bespake the school-master,
>Unto the lord of Learne said he,
>'I think thou be some stranger born,
>For the Holy Ghost remains with thee.'

4.
>He said, 'I am no stranger born,
>Forsooth, master, I tell it to thee,
>It is a gift of Almighty God
>Which He hath given unto me.'

5.
>The school-master turn'd him round about,
>His angry mind he thought to assuage,
>For the child could answer him so quickly,
>And was of so tender year of age.

6.
>The child, he caused a steed to be brought,
>A golden bridle done him upon;
>He took his leave of his schoolfellows,
>And home the child that he is gone.

7.
    And when he came before his father,
    He fell low down upon his knee,
    'My blessing, father, I would ask,
    If Christ would grant you would give it me.'

8.
    'Now God thee bless, my son and my heir,
    His servant in heaven that thou may be!
    What tidings hast thou brought me, child,
    Thou art comen home so soon to me?'

9.
    9.² The line is partly cut away in the MS.: I follow the suggestion of Hales and Furnivall.
    'Good tidings, father, I have you brought,
    Good tidings I hope it is to me;
    The book is not in all Scotland,
    But I can read it before your eye.'

10.
    10.⁴ In the MS. the line stands: 'To learn the speeches of all strange lands.'
    A joyed man his father was,
    Even the worthy lord of Learne;
    'Thou shalt go into France, my child,
    The speeches of all strange lands to learn.'

11.
    But then bespake the child his mother—
    The lady of Learne and then was she—
    Says, 'Who must be his well good guide,
    When he goes into that strange country?'

12.
    12.³ 'hend,' kindly, friendly.
    And then bespake that bonny child
    Untill his father tenderly,
    Says, 'Father, I'll have the hend steward,
    For he hath been true to you and me.'

13.
    13.⁴ 'mere' = more.
    The lady to counsel the steward did take,
    And counted down a hundred pounds there,
    Says, 'Steward, be true to my son and my heir,
    And I will give thee mickle mere.'

14.
>'If I be not true to my master,' he said,
>'Christ himself be not true to me!
>If I be not true to my lord and master,
>An ill death that I may die!'

15.
>The lord of Learne did apparel his child
>With brooch, and ring, and many a thing;
>The apparel he had his body upon,
>They say was worth a squire's living.

16.
>The parting of the young lord of Learne
>With his father, his mother, his fellows dear,
>Would have made a man's heart for to change,
>If a Jew born that he were.

17.
>The wind did serve, and they did sail
>Over the sea into France land:
>He used the child so hardly,
>He would let him have never a penny to spend.

18.
>And meat he would let the child have none,
>Nor money to buy none truly;
>The boy was hungry and thirsty both;
>Alas! it was the more pity.

19.
>He laid him down to drink the water
>That was so low beneath the brim;
>He was wont to have drunk both ale and wine,
>Then was fain of the water so thin.

20.
>And as he was drinking of the water
>That ran so low beneath the brim,
>So ready was the false steward
>To drown the bonny boy therein.

21.
>21.² 'lend,' grant.
>'Have mercy on me, worthy steward!
>My life,' he said, 'lend it to me!
>And all that I am heir upon,'
>Says, 'I will give unto thee.'

22.
>22.³ 'Even,' MS.

Mercy to him the steward did take,
And pull'd the child out of the brim;
Ever alack! the more pity,
He took his clothes even from him.

23.

> 23.¹ etc. 'Do thou off,' take off.
> 23.³ 'cordivant' = cordwain, leather from Cordova, in Spain. See *Brown Robin*, 17.⁴, First Series, p. 161.

Says, 'Do thou me off that velvet gown,
The crimson hose beneath thy knee,
And do me off thy cordivant shoon
Are buckled with the gold so free.

24.

'Do thou me off thy satin doublet,
Thy shirtband wrought with glistering gold,
And do me off thy golden chain
About thy neck so many a fold.

25.

> 25.⁴ 'Seam': Child's emendation, adopted from the broadside copies, for 'swain' in the MS.

'Do thou me off thy velvet hat
With feather in that is so fine,
All unto thy silken shirt
That's wrought with many a golden seam.'

26.

The child before him naked stood,
With skin as white as lily flower;
For his worthy lord's beauty
He might have been a lady's paramour.

27.

He put upon him a leather coat,
And breeches of the same beneath the knee,
And sent that bonny child him fro,
Service for to crave, truly.

28.

He pull'd then forth a naked sword
That hange[d] full low then by his side,
'Turn thy name, thou villain,' he said,
'Or else this sword shall be thy guide.'

29.

'What must be my name, worthy steward?
I pray thee now tell it me.'
'Thy name shall be poor Disaware,

30.
    To tend sheep on a lonely lea.'

31.
    The bonny child, he went him fro,
    And looked to himself truly,
    Saw his apparel so simple upon;
    O Lord! he weeped tenderly.

32.
    Unto a shepherd's house that child did go,
    And said, 'Sir, God you save and see!
    Do you not want a servant boy
    To tend your sheep on a lonely lea?'

33.
    'Where was thou born?' the shepherd said,
    'Where, my boy, or in what country?'
    'Sir,' he said, 'I was born in fair Scotland
    That is so far beyond the sea.'

34.
    'I have no child,' the shepherd said,
    'My boy, thou'st tarry and dwell with me;
    My living,' he said, 'and all my goods,
    I'll make thee heir [of] after me.'

35.
    And then bespake the shepherd's wife,
    To the lord of Learne thus did she say,
    'Go thy way to our sheep,' she said,
    'And tend them well both night and day.'

36.
    It was a sore office, O Lord, for him
    That was a lord born of a great degree!
    As he was tending his sheep alone,
    Neither sport nor play could he.

37.
    Let us leave talking of the lord of Learne,
    And let all such talking go;
    Let us talk more of the false steward
    That caused the child all this woe.

38.
    37.[2] The last word added by Child: ep. 43.[3], 104.[2].
    He sold this lord of Learne his clothes
    For five hundred pounds to his pay [there],
    And bought himself a suit of apparel,
    Might well beseem a lord to wear.

When he that gorgeous apparel bought
That did so finely his body upon,
He laughed the bonny child to scorn
That was the bonny lord of Learne.

39.

39.[4] A popular proverb.
He laughed that bonny boy to scorne;
Lord! pity it was to hear!
I have heard them say, and so have you too,
That a man may buy gold too dear.

40.

When that he had all that gorgeous apparel
That did so finely his body upon,
He went a wooing to the duke's daughter of France,
And called himself the lord of Learne.

41.

The duke of France heard tell of this;
To his place that worthy lord was come truly;
He entertain'd him with a quart of red Rhenish wine.
Says, 'Lord of Learne, thou art welcome to me!'

42.

42.[4] Cp. the horror of 'churlës blood' in *Glasgerion*, 9.[5,6] (First Series, p. 5).
Then to supper that they were set,
Lords and ladies in their degree;
The steward was set next the duke of France;
An unseemly sight it was to see.

43.

Then bespake the duke of France,
Unto the lord of Learne said he there,
Says, 'Lord of Learne, if thou'll marry my daughter,
I'll mend thy living five hundred pounds a year.'

44.

Then bespake that lady fair,
Answered her father so alone,
That she would be his married wife
If he would make her Lady of Learne.

45.

Then hand in hand the steward her he took,
And plight that lady his troth alone,
That she should be his married wife,
And he would make her the lady of Learne.

46.

Thus that night it was gone,

The other day was come truly.
The lady would see the roe-buck run
Up hills and dales and forest free.

47.
Then she was ware of the young lord of Learne
Tending sheep under a briar, truly;
And thus she called unto her maids,
And held her hands up thus on high,
Says, 'Fetch me yond shepherd's boy,
I'll know why he doth mourn, truly.'

48.
When he came before that lady fair
He fell down upon his knee;
He had been so well brought up
He needed not to learn courtesy.

49.
'Where wast thou born, thou bonny boy,
Where or in what country?'
'Madam, I was born in fair Scotland,
That is so far beyond the sea.'

50.
'What is thy name, thou bonny boy?
I pray thee tell it unto me.'
'My name,' he says, 'is poor Disaware,
That tends sheep on a lonely lea.'

51.
'One thing thou must tell me, bonny boy,
Which I must needs ask of thee:
Dost not thou know the young lord of Learne?
He is come a wooing into France to me.'

52.
'Yes, that I do, madam,' he said;
And then he wept most tenderly;
'The lord of Learne is a worthy lord,
If he were at home in his own country.'

53.
'What ails thee to weep, my bonny boy?
Tell me or ere I part thee fro.'
'Nothing but for a friend, madam,
That's dead from me many a year ago.'

54.
A loud laughter the lady laughed;
O Lord, she smiled wondrous high;

'I have dwelled in France since I was born;
Such a shepherd's boy I did never see.

55.
    'Wilt thou not leave thy sheep, my child,
    And come unto service unto me?
    And I will give thee meat and fee,
    And my chamberlain thou shalt be.'

56.
    'Then I will leave my sheep, madam,' he said,
    'And come into service unto thee;
    If you will give me meat and fee,
    Your chamberlain that I may be.'

57.
    When the lady came before her father,
    She fell low down upon her knee;
    'Grant me, father,' the lady said,
    'This boy my chamberlain to be.'

58.
    'But O nay, nay,' the duke did say,
    'So, my daughter, it may not be;
    The lord that is come a wooing to you
    Will be offended with you and me.'

59.
    Then came down the false steward
    Which called himself the lord of Learne, truly:
    When he looked that bonny boy upon,
    An angry man i-wis was he.

60.
    60.[1] 'Where thou was,' MS.
    'Where was thou born, thou vagabond?
    'Where?' he said, 'and in what country?'
    Says, 'I was born in fair Scotland
    That is so far beyond the sea.'

61.
    'What is thy name, thou vagabond?
    Have done quickly, and tell it to me.'
    'My name,' he says, 'is poor Disaware;
    I tend sheep on the lonely lea.'
    'Thou art a thief,' the steward said,
    'And so in the end I will prove thee.'

62.
    Then bespake the lady fair,
    'Peace, lord of Learne! I do pray thee;

For if no love you show this child,
No favour can you have of me.'

63.

63.⁴ The MS. reads '... robbed a 100: 3,'
'Will you believe me, lady fair,
When the truth I do tell ye?
At Aberdonie beyond the sea
His father he robbed a hundred [and] three.'

64.

But then bespake the duke of France
Unto the boy so tenderly,
Says, 'Boy, if thou love horses well,
My stable groom I will make thee.'

65.

And thus that that did pass upon
Till the twelve months did draw to an end;
The boy applied his office so well,
Every man became his friend.

66.

He went forth early one morning
To water a gelding at the water so free;
The gelding up, and with his head
He hit the child above his eye.

67.

67.⁴ 'eye': the MS. gives *knee*.
'Woe be to thee, thou gelding!' he said,
'And to the mare that foaled thee!
Thou has stricken the lord of Learne
A little tiny above the eye.

68.

68.¹ 'after' is superfluous (cp. 74.¹), and is probably caught up from the next line.
'First night after I was born, a lord I was;
An earl after my father doth die;
My father is the worthy lord of Learne;
His child he hath no more but me;
He sent me over the sea with the false steward,
And thus that he hath beguiled me.'

69.

The lady [wa]s in her garden green,
Walking with her maids, truly,
And heard the boy this mourning make,
And went to weeping truly.

70.
>70.² 'let,' stop.
>'Sing on thy song, thou stable groom,
>I pray thee do not let for me,
>And as I am a true lady
>I will be true unto thee.'

71.
>'But nay, now nay, madam!' he said,
>'So that it may not be,
>I am ta'en sworn upon a book,
>And forsworn I will not be.'

72.
>'Sing on thy song to thy gelding
>And thou dost not sing to me;
>And as I am a true lady
>I will ever be true unto thee.'

73.
>He said, 'Woe be to thee, gelding,
>And to the mare that foaled thee!
>For thou hast stricken the lord of Learne
>A little above mine eye.

74.
>'First night I was born, a lord I was;
>An earl after my father doth die;
>My father is the good lord of Learne,
>And child he hath no other but me.
>My father sent me over with the false steward,
>And thus that he hath beguiled me.

75.
>'Woe be to the steward, lady,' he said,
>'Woe be to him verily!
>He hath been above this twelve months' day
>For to deceive both thee and me.

76.
>'If you do not my counsel keep
>That I have told you with good intent,
>And if you do it not well keep,
>Farewell! my life is at an end.'

77.
>'I will be true to thee, lord of Learne,
>Or else Christ be not so unto me;
>And as I am a true lady,
>I'll never marry none but thee!'

78.

> 78.⁴, 79.⁴ 'these': the MS. gives *this* in each instance: 'months' is probably to be read as a dissyllable, either as 'moneths' or 'monthës.'
> She sent in for her father, the duke,
> In all the speed that e'er might be;
> 'Put off my wedding, father,' she said,
> 'For the love of God, these months three.

79.

> 'Sick I am,' the lady said,
> 'O sick, and very like to die!
> Put off my wedding, father duke,
> For the love of God, these months three.'

80.

> The duke of France put off this wedding
> Of the steward and the lady, months three;
> For the lady sick she was,
> Sick, sick, and like to die.

81.

> She wrote a letter with her own hand,
> In all the speed that ever might be;
> She sent over into Scotland
> That is so far beyond the sea.

82.

> When the messenger came before the old lord of Learne,
> He kneeled low down on his knee,
> And he delivered the letter unto him
> In all the speed that ever might be.

83.

> First look he looked the letter upon,
> Lo! he wept full bitterly;
> The second look he looked it upon,
> Said, 'False steward! woe be to thee!'

84.

> When the lady of Learne these tidings heard,
> O Lord! she wept so bitterly:
> 'I told you of this, now good my lord,
> When I sent my child into that wild country.'

85.

> 85.⁴ 'Wroken,' avenged.
> 'Peace, lady of Learne,' the lord did say,
> 'For Christ his love I do pray thee;
> And as I am a Christian man,
> Wroken upon him that I will be.'

86.
>He wrote a letter with his own hand
>In all the speed that e'er might be;
>He sent it into the lords in Scotland
>That were born of a great degree.

87.
>He sent for lords, he sent for knights,
>The best that were in the country,
>To go with him into the land of France,
>To seek his son in that strange country.

88.
>The wind was good, and they did sail,
>Five hundred men into France land,
>There to seek that bonny boy
>That was the worthy lord of Learne.

89.
>They sought the country through and through,
>So far to the duke's place of France land:
>There they were ware of that bonny boy
>Standing with a porter's staff in his hand.

90.
>Then the worshipful they did bow,
>The serving-men fell on their knee,
>They cast their hats up into the air
>For joy that boy that they did see.

91.
>The lord of Learne, then he light down,
>And kissed his child both cheek and chin,
>And said, 'God bless thee, my son and my heir,
>The bliss of heaven that thou may win!'

92.
>The false steward and the duke of France
>Were in a castle top truly:
>'What fools are yond,' says the false steward,
>'To the porter makes so low courtesy?'

93.
>Then bespake the duke of France,
>Calling my lord of Learne truly,
>He said, 'I doubt the day be come
>That either you or I must die.'

94.
>They set the castle round about,
>A swallow could not have flown away;

    And there they took the false steward
    That the lord of Learne did betray.

95.

    And when they had taken the false steward,
    He fell low down upon his knee,
    And craved mercy of the lord of Learne
    For the villainous deed he had done, truly.

96.

    'Thou shalt have mercy,' said the lord of Learne,
    'Thou vile traitor! I tell to thee,
    As the laws of the realm they will thee bear,
    Whether it be for thee to live or die.'

97.

    A quest of lords that there was chosen
    To go upon his death, truly:
    There they judged the false steward,
    Whether he was guilty, and for to die.

98.

    The foreman of the jury, he came in;
    He spake his words full loud and high:
    Said, 'Make thee ready, thou false steward,
    For now thy death it draws full nigh!'

99.

    Said he, 'If my death it doth draw nigh,
    God forgive me all I have done amiss!
    Where is that lady I have loved so long,
    Before my death to give me a kiss?'

100.

    'Away, thou traitor!' the lady said,
    'Avoid out of my company!
    For thy vile treason thou hast wrought,
    Thou had need to cry to God for mercy.'

101.

    101.[4] 'sod,' soused: cp. *The Two Noble Kinsmen*, I.3, line 21; 'lead,' cauldron: cp. *The Maid and the Palmer*, 9.[2], p. 154. 'Salting-leads' are still in use.
    First they took him and hang'd him half,
    And let him down before he was dead,
    And quartered him in quarters many,
    And sod him in a boiling lead.

102.

    And then they took him out again,
    And cutten all his joints in sunder,
    And burnt him eke upon a hill;

I-wis they did him curstly cumber.

103.
A loud laughter the lady laughed;
O Lord! she smiled merrily;
She said, 'I may praise my heavenly King,
That ever I seen this vile traitor die.'

104.
104.⁴ 'pounds' inserted to agree with 43.⁴.
Then bespake the duke of France,
Unto the right lord of Learne said he there,
Says, 'Lord of Learne, if thou wilt marry my daughter,
I'll mend thy living five hundred [pounds] a year.'

105.
But then bespake that bonny boy,
And answered the duke quickly,
'I had rather marry your daughter with a ring of gold,
Than all the gold that e'er I blinked on with mine eye.'

106.
But then bespake the old lord of Learne,
To the duke of France thus he did say,
'Seeing our children do so well agree,
They shall be married ere we go away.'

107.
The lady of Learne, she was for sent
Throughout Scotland so speedily,
To see these two children set up
In their seats of gold full royally.

THE BAILIFF'S DAUGHTER OF ISLINGTON

THE TEXT is formed by a collation of six broadsides printed between 1672 and 1700: they do not, however, present many variations. Here, if anywhere, one would demand licence to make alterations and improvements. In stanza 12 the rhymes are almost certainly misplaced; and the last stanza is quite superfluous. It would be much more in keeping with ballad-style to end with the twelfth, and many of the variants now sung conclude thus. This ballad is still extremely popular, and not only has it been included in many selections and song-books, but it is also still in oral tradition.

THE STORY is simple and pre-eminently in the popular vein. Counterparts exist elsewhere in the languages derived from Latin, and in Romaic.

THE BAILIFF'S DAUGHTER OF ISLINGTON

1.
    THERE was a youth, and a well-belov'd youth,
    And he was a squire's son,
    He loved the bailiff's daughter dear,
    That lived in Islington.

2.
    She was coy, and she would not believe
    That he did love her so,
    No, nor at any time she would
    Any countenance to him show.

3.
    But when his friends did understand
    His fond and foolish mind,
    They sent him up to fair London,
    An apprentice for to bind.

4.
    And when he had been seven long years,
    And his love he had not seen,
    'Many a tear have I shed for her sake
    When she little thought of me.'

5.
>All the maids of Islington
>Went forth to sport and play;
>All but the bailiff's daughter dear;
>She secretly stole away.

6.
>6.[2] 'puggish.' 'Pugging' means 'thieving,' and J. W. Ebsworth suggests that here it implies ragged clothing, like a tramp's.
>She put off her gown of gray,
>And put on her puggish attire;
>She's up to fair London gone,
>Her true-love to require.

7.
>As she went along the road,
>The weather being hot and dry,
>There was she aware of her true-love,
>At length came riding by.

8.
>8.[2] Five of the broadsides give 'bridal ring.'
>She stept to him, as red as any rose,
>And took him by the bridle-ring:
>'I pray you, kind sir, give me one penny,
>To ease my weary limb.'

9.
>'I prithee, sweetheart, canst thou tell me
>Where that thou wast born?'
>'At Islington, kind sir,' said she,
>'Where I have had many a scorn.'

10.
>'I prithee, sweetheart, canst thou tell me
>Whether thou dost know
>The bailiff's daughter of Islington?'
>'She's dead, sir, long ago.'

11.
>'Then I will sell my goodly steed,
>My saddle and my bow;
>I will into some far country,
>Where no man doth me know.'

12.
    'O stay, O stay, thou goodly youth!
    She's alive, she is not dead;
    Here she standeth by thy side,
    And is ready to be thy bride.'

13.
    'O farewell grief, and welcome joy,
    Ten thousand times and more!
    For now I have seen my own true love,
    That I thought I should have seen no more.'

GLENLOGIE

THE TEXT is from Sharpe's *Ballad Book* (1823). It is an extremely popular ballad in Scotland.

THE STORY.—Lady Jean Melville (in other versions Jean of Bethelnie, in Aberdeenshire), scarce sixteen years old, falls in love at first sight with Glenlogie, and tells him her mind. But he is already engaged, and Lady Jean takes to her care-bed. Her father offers the consolation, usual in such cases, of another and a richer husband. Jean, however, prefers the love of Glenlogie to the euphony of Drumfendrich, and gets her father's chaplain to write a letter to Glenlogie, which is so well indited that it moves him to tears, and all ends happily.

GLENLOGIE

1.
    FOUR and twenty nobles sits in the king's ha',
    Bonnie Glenlogie is the flower among them a'.

2.
    In came Lady Jean, skipping on the floor,
    And she has chosen Glenlogie 'mong a' that was there.

3.
    She turned to his footman, and thus she did say:
    'Oh, what is his name? and where does he stay?'

4.
    'His name is Glenlogie, when he is from home;
    He is of the gay Gordons, his name it is John.'

5.
    'Glenlogie, Glenlogie, an you will prove kind,
    My love is laid on you; I am telling my mind.'

6.
    He turned about lightly, as the Gordons does a':
    'I thank you, Lady Jean, my loves is promised awa'.'

7.
    She called on her maidens her bed for to make,
    Her rings and her jewels all from her to take.

8.
    In came Jeanie's father, a wae man was he;
    Says, 'I'll wed you to Drumfendrich, he has mair gold than he.'

9.

> Her father's own chaplain, being a man of great skill,
> He wrote him a letter, and indited it well.

10.
> The first lines he looked at, a light laugh laughed he;
> But ere he read through it the tears blinded his e'e.

11.
> Oh, pale and wan looked she when Glenlogie cam in.
> But even rosy grew she when Glenlogie sat down.

12.
> 'Turn round, Jeanie Melville, turn round to this side,
> And I'll be the bridegroom, and you'll be the bride.'

13.
> Oh, 'twas a merry wedding, and the portion down told,
> Of bonnie Jeanie Melville, who was scarce sixteen years old.

KING ORFEO

THE TEXT was derived from Mr. Biot Edmondston's memory of a ballad sung to him by an old man in Unst, Shetland. In the version sung, he notes, there were no stanzas to fill the obvious gap in the story after the first; but that after the fourth and the eighth stanzas, there had been certain verses which he had forgotten. In the first instance, these related that the lady had been carried off by fairies, and that the king, going in search of her, saw her one day among a company that passed into a castle on the hillside. After the eighth stanza, the ballad related that a messenger appeared behind the grey stone, and invited the king in.

The refrain is a startling instance of phonetic tradition, the words being repeated by rote long after the sense has been forgotten. It appears that the two lines are Unst pronunciation of Danish, and that they mean, respectively, 'Early green's the wood,' and 'Where the hart goes yearly.'

In this connection, compare Arthur Edmondston's *A View of the Ancient and Present State of the Zetland Islands* (1809), vol. i. p. 142: 'The island of Unst was its [pure Norse] last abode; and not more than thirty years ago several individuals there could speak it fluently.' See also Rev. Dr. Barry's *History of the Orkney Islands* (1805), Appendix No. X., pp. 484-490, a ballad of thirty-five quatrains in Norse as spoken in the Orkneys, the subject of which is a contest between a King of Norway and an Earl of Orkney, who had married the King's daughter, in her father's absence, and without his consent.

THE STORY.—Doubtless few will recognise in this fragment an offshoot of the classical story of Orpheus and Eurydice. The ballad, however, cannot be said to be derived directly from the classical tale: rather it represents the *débris* of the mediæval romance of *Orfeo and Heurodis*, where the kingdom of Faëry (see 4.¹) replaces Hades, and the tale is given a happy ending by the recovery of Eurydice (for whom the Lady Isabel is here the substitute). The romance exists as *Orfeo and Heurodis* in the Auchinleck MS., of the fourteenth century, in the Advocates' Library, Edinburgh; as *Kyng Orfew* in Ashmole MS. 61, of the fifteenth century; and as *Sir Orpheo* in Harleian MS. 3810.

KING ORFEO

1.
   DER lived a king inta da aste,
   Scowan ürla grün
   Der lived a lady in da wast.
   Whar giorten han grün oarlac

2.
   Dis king he has a huntin' gaen,
   He's left his Lady Isabel alane.

3.
   'Oh I wis ye'd never gaen away,
   For at your hame is döl an' wae.

4.
   'For da king o' Ferrie we his daert,
   Has pierced your lady to da hert.'
   *   *   *   *   *

5.
   And aifter dem da king has gaen,
   But whan he cam it was a grey stane.

6.
   Dan he took oot his pipes ta play,
   Bit sair his hert wi' döl an' wae.

7.
   7.[1] 'noy,' grief.
   And first he played da notes o' noy,
   An' dan he played da notes o' joy.

8.
   8.[1] 'The good gabber reel' is a sprightly dance-tune.
   An' dan he played da göd gabber reel,
   Dat meicht ha' made a sick hert hale.
   *   *   *   *   *

9.
   9.[1,2] 'wir,' 'wis,' our, us.
   'Noo come ye in inta wir ha',
   An' come ye in among wis a'.'

10.
    Now he's gaen in inta der ha',
    An' he's gaen in among dem a'.

11.
    Dan he took out his pipes to play,
    Bit sair his hert wi' döl an' wae.

12.
    An' first he played da notes o' noy,
    An' dan he played da notes o' joy.
13.
    An' dan he played da göd gabber reel,
    Dat meicht ha' made a sick hert hale.
14.
    'Noo tell to us what ye will hae:
    What sall we gie you for your play?'
15.
    'What I will hae I will you tell,
    And dat's me Lady Isabel.'
16.
    'Yees tak your lady, an' yees gaeng hame,
    An' yees be king ower a' your ain.'
17.
    He's taen his lady, an' he's gaen hame,
    An' noo he's king ower a' his ain.

THE BAFFLED KNIGHT

THE TEXT is from Ravenscroft's *Deuteromelia* (1609), reprinted almost *verbatim* in Tom Durfey's *Pills to Purge Melancholy*.

THE STORY was sufficiently popular not only to have been revived, at the end of the seventeenth century, but to have had three other 'Parts' added to it, the whole four afterwards being combined into one broadside.

In similar Spanish, Portuguese, and French ballads, the damsel escapes by saying she is a leper, or the daughter of a leper, or otherwise diseased. Much the same story is told in Danish and German ballads.

THE BAFFLED KNIGHT

1.
>1.² 'lay' = lea, meadow-land.
>YONDER comes a courteous knight,
>Lustely raking over the lay;
>He was well ware of a bonny lasse,
>As she came wand'ring over the way.
>*Then she sang downe a downe, hey downe derry   (bis)*

2.
>'Jove you speed, fayre ladye,' he said,
>'Among the leaves that be so greene;
>If I were a king, and wore a crowne,
>Full soone, fair lady, shouldst thou be a queen.

3.
>'Also Jove save you, faire lady,
>Among the roses that be so red;
>If I have not my will of you,
>Full soone, faire lady, shall I be dead.'

4.
>4.⁴ 'divel's mouth.' Skeat has suggested that this metaphor is derived from the devil's mouth always being wide open in painted windows.
>Then he lookt east, then hee lookt west,
>Hee lookt north, so did he south;
>He could not finde a privy place,
>For all lay in the divel's mouth.

5.
>'If you will carry me, gentle sir,
>A mayde unto my father's hall,

      Then you shall have your will of me,
      Under purple and under paule.'

6.

      He set her up upon a steed,
      And him selfe upon another,
      And all the day he rode her by,
      As though they had been sister and brother.

7.

      7.[3] 'yode,' went.
      7.[4] 'foure-ear'd.' Child suggests, 'as denoting a double ass?'
      When she came to her father's hall,
      It was well walled round about;
      She yode in at the wicket-gate,
      And shut the foure-ear'd foole without.

8.

      'You had me,' quoth she, 'abroad in the field,
      Among the corne, amidst the hay,
      Where you might had your will of mee,
      For, in good faith, sir, I never said nay.

9.

      'Ye had me also amid the field,
      Among the rushes that were so browne,
      Where you might had your will of me,
      But you had not the face to lay me downe.'

10.

      10.[1,2] See First Series, Introduction, p. xlix.
      He pulled out his nut-browne sword,
      And wipt the rust off with his sleeve,
      And said, 'Jove's curse come to his heart,
      That any woman would beleeve!'

11.

      When you have your own true-love
      A mile or twaine out of the towne,
      Spare not for her gay clothing,
      But lay her body flat on the ground.

OUR GOODMAN

THE TEXT is from Herd's MSS., as given by Professor Child to form a regular sequence. The ballad also exists in an English broadside form.

THE STORY of the ballad has a close counterpart in Flemish Belgium, and in southern France. The German variants, however, have a curious history. The English broadside ballad was translated into German by F. W. Meyer in 1789, and in this form gained such popularity that it was circulated not only as a broadside, but actually in oral tradition,—with the usual result of alteration. Its vogue was not confined to Germany, but spread to Hungary and Scandinavia, a Swedish broadside appearing within ten years of Meyer's translation.

OUR GOODMAN

1.
>HAME came our goodman,
>And hame came he,
>And then he saw a saddle-horse,
>Where nae horse should be.

2.
>'What's this now, goodwife?
>What's this I see?
>How came this horse here,
>Without the leave o' me?'
>*Recitative.*
>'A horse?' quo' she.
>'Ay, a horse,' quo' he.

3.
>3.² 'mat,' may.
>3.³ 'broad,' brood: *i.e.* a sow that has a litter.
>3.⁴ 'minnie,' mother.
>'Shame fa' your cuckold face,
>Ill mat ye see!
>'Tis naething but a broad sow,
>My minnie sent to me.'
>'A broad sow?' quo' he.
>'Ay, a sow,' quo' shee.

4.
    'Far hae I ridden,
    And farer hae I gane,
    But a saddle on a sow's back
    I never saw nane.'

5.
    Hame came our goodman,
    And hame came he;
    He spy'd a pair of jack-boots,
    Where nae boots should be.

6.
    'What's this now, goodwife?
    What's this I see?
    How came these boots here,
    Without the leave o' me?'
    'Boots?' quo' she.
    'Ay, boots,' quo' he.

7.
    'Shame fa' your cuckold face,
    And ill mat ye see!
    It's but a pair of water-stoups,
    My minnie sent to me.'
    'Water-stoups?' quo' he.
    'Ay, water-stoups,' quo' she.

8.
    'Far hae I ridden,
    And farer hae I gane,
    But siller spurs on water-stoups
    I saw never nane.'

9.
    Hame came our goodman,
    And hame came he,
    And he saw a sword,
    Whare a sword should na be.

10.
    'What's this now, goodwife?
    What's this I see?
    How came this sword here,
    Without the leave o' me?'
    'A sword?' quo' she.
    'Ay, a sword,' quo' he.

11.
>11.³ 'porridge-spurtle,' stick for stirring porridge.
>'Shame fa' your cuckold face,
>Ill mat ye see!
>It's but a porridge-spurtle,
>My minnie sent to me.'
>'A spurtle?' quo' he.
>'Ay, a spurtle,' quo' she.

12.
>'Far hae I ridden,
>And farer hae I gane,
>But siller-handed spurtles
>I saw never nane.'

13.
>Hame came our goodman,
>And hame came he;
>There he spy'd a powder'd wig,
>Where nae wig shoud be.

14.
>'What's this now, goodwife?
>What's this I see?
>How came this wig here,
>Without the leave o' me?'
>'A wig?' quo' she.
>'Ay, a wig,' quo' he.

15.
>15.³ 'clocken-hen,' sitting hen.
>'Shame fa' your cuckold face,
>And ill mat you see!
>'Tis naething but a clocken-hen,
>My minnie sent to me.'
>'Clocken hen?' quo' he.
>'Ay, clocken hen,' quo' she.

16.
>'Far hae I ridden,
>And farer hae I gane,
>But powder on a clocken-hen
>I saw never nane.'

17.
>Hame came our goodman,
>And hame came he,
>And there he saw a muckle coat,
>Where nae coat shoud be.

18.
    'What's this now, goodwife?
    What's this I see?
    How came this coat here,
    Without the leave o' me?'
    'A coat?' quo' she.
    'Ay, a coat,' quo' he.

19.
    'Shame fa' your cuckold face,
    Ill mat ye see!
    It's but a pair o' blankets,
    My minnie sent to me.'
    'Blankets?' quo' he.
    'Ay, blankets,' quo' she.

20.
    'Far hae I ridden,
    And farer hae I gane,
    But buttons upon blankets
    I saw never nane.'

21.
    21.[1] 'Ben,' indoors, or into the inner room.
    Ben went our goodman,
    And ben went he,
    And there he spy'd a sturdy man,
    Where nae man shoud be.

22.
    'What's this now, goodwife?
    What's this I see?
    How came this man here,
    Without the leave o' me?'
    'A man?' quo' she.
    'Ay, a man,' quo' he.

23.
    'Poor blind body,
    And blinder mat ye be!
    It's a new milking-maid,
    My mither sent to me.'
    'A maid?' quo' he.
    'Ay, a maid,' quo' she.

24.
    'Far hae I ridden,
    And farer hae I gane,
    But lang-bearded maidens
    I saw never nane.'

THE FRIAR IN THE WELL

THE TEXT is taken from Buchan's MSS., the Scots version being rather more condensed than the corresponding English broadside. There is a reference to this ballad in Munday's *Downfall of Robert, Earl of Huntington* (1598); but earlier still, Skelton hints at it in *Colyn Cloute*.

THE STORY can be paralleled in French, Danish, and Persian ballads and tales, but is simple enough to have been invented by almost any people. Compare also the story of *The Wright's Chaste Wife* by Adam of Cobsam, E.E.T.S., 1865, ed. F. J. Furnivall.

THE FRIAR IN THE WELL

1.
>1.2,4 The burden is of course repeated in each stanza.
>O HEARKEN and hear, and I will you tell
>*Sing, Faldidae, faldidadi*
>Of a friar that loved a fair maiden well.
>*Sing, Faldi dadi di di*   (*bis*)

2.
>The friar he came to this maiden's bedside,
>And asking for her maidenhead.

3.
>'O I would grant you your desire,
>If 't werena for fear o' hell's burning fire.'

4.
>'O' hell's burning fire ye need have no doubt;
>Altho' you were in, I could whistle you out.'

5.
>'O if I grant to you this thing,
>Some money you unto me must bring.'

6.
>He brought her the money, and did it down tell;
>She had a white cloth spread over the well.

7.
>Then the fair maid cried out that her master was come;
>'O,' said the friar,' then where shall I run?'

8.
>'O ye will go in behind yon screen,
>And then by my master ye winna be seen.'

9.
>Then in behind the screen she him sent,
>But he fell into the well by accident.

10.
>Then the friar cried out with a piteous moan,
>'O help! O help me! or else I am gone.'

11.
>'Ye said ye wad whistle me out o' hell;
>Now whistle your ain sel' out o' the well.'

12.
>She helped him out and bade him be gone;
>The friar he asked his money again.

13.
>'As for your money, there is no much matter
>To make you pay more for jumbling our water.'

14.
>Then all who hear it commend this fair maid
>For the nimble trick to the friar she played.

15.
>15.[2] 'lugs,' ears.
>The friar he walked on the street,
>And shaking his lugs like a well-washen sheep.

THE KNIGHT AND THE SHEPHERD'S DAUGHTER

THE TEXT is given here from Kinloch's MSS. He gives also three other versions and various fragments. The tale is also found amongst the Roxburghe Ballads, as *The Beautifull Shepherdesse of Arcadia*, in two broadsides printed about 1655 and 1680. This is the only English version extant. But earlier than any text of the ballad is a quotation from it in John Fletcher's *The Pilgrim*, iv. 2 (1621). The Scots versions, about a dozen in number, are far more lively than the broadside. Buchan printed two, of sixty and sixty-three stanzas respectively. Another text is delightfully inconsequent:—

> "'Some ca' me Jack, some ca' me John,
>
> Some ca' me Jing-ga-lee,
>
> But when I am in the queen's court
>
> Earl Hitchcock they ca' me."
>
> "Hitchcock, Hitchcock," Jo Janet she said,
>
> An' spelled it ower agane,
>
> "Hitchcock it's a Latin word;
>
> Earl Richard is your name."
>
> But when he saw she was book-learned,
>
> Fast to his horse hied he....'

Both this version (from the Gibb MS.) and one of Buchan's introduce the domestic genius known as the 'Billy-Blin,' for whom see *Young Bekie*, First Series, p. 6, ff.; *Willie's Lady*, p. 19 of this volume; and *Cospatrick*, p. 26.

THE STORY.—The King of France's auld dochter, disguised as a shepherdess, is accosted by Sweet William, brother to the Queen of Scotland, who gives his name as Wilfu' Will, varied by Jack and John. He attempts to escape, but she follows him to court, and claims him in marriage from the king. He tries to avoid discovery by pretending to be a cripple, but she knows him, refuses to be bribed, marries him, and finally reveals herself to him.

The *dénouement* of the story is reminiscent of *The Marriage of Sir Gawain* (First Series, pp. 107-118). A Danish ballad, *Ebbe Galt*, has similar incidents.

THE KNIGHT AND THE SHEPHERD'S DAUGHTER

1.
    THERE was a shepherd's dochter
    Kept sheep upon yon hill,
    And by cam a gay braw gentleman,
    And wad hae had his will.

2.
    He took her by the milk-white hand,
    And laid her on the ground,
    And whan he got his will o' her
    He lift her up again.

3.
    'O syne ye've got your will o' me,
    Your will o' me ye've taen,
    'Tis all I ask o' you, kind sir,
    Is to tell to me your name.'

4.
    'Sometimes they call me Jack,' he said,
    'Sometimes they call me John,
    But whan I am in the king's court,
    My name is Wilfu' Will.'

5.
    Than he loup on his milk-white steed,
    And straught away he rade,
    And she did kilt her petticoats,
    And after him she gaed.

6.
    He never was sae kind as say,
    'O lassie, will ye ride?'
    Nor ever had she the courage to say,
    'O laddie, will ye bide!'

7.
    Until they cam to a wan water,
    Which was called Clyde,
    And then he turned about his horse,
    Said, 'Lassie, will ye ride?'

8.
    8.² 'weel,' advantage. So, in the comparative, 'better,' 9.².
    'I learned it in my father's hall,
    I learned it for my weel,
    That whan I come to deep water,

I can swim as it were an eel.

9.
'I learned it in my mother's bower,
I learned it for my better,
That whan I come to broad water,
I can swim like any otter.'

10.
He plunged his steed into the ford,
And straught way thro' he rade,
And she set in her lilly feet,
And thro' the water wade.

11.
And whan she cam to the king's court,
She tirled on the pin,
And wha sae ready's the king himsel'
To let the fair maid in?

12.
'What is your will wi' me, fair maid?
What is your will wi' me?'
'There is a man into your court
This day has robbed me.'

13.
'O has he taen your gold,' he said,
'Or has he taen your fee?
Or has he stown your maidenhead,
The flower of your bodye?'

14.
'He has na taen my gold, kind sir,
Nor as little has he taen my fee,
But he has taen my maidenhead,
The flower of my bodye.'

15.
'O gif he be a married man,
High hangit shall he be,
But gif he be a bachelor,
His body I'll grant thee.'

16.
'Sometimes they call him Jack,' she said,
'Sometimes they call him John,
But when he's in the king's court,
His name is Sweet William.'

17.
    'There's not a William in a' my court,
    Never a one but three,
    And one of them is the Queen's brother;
    I wad laugh gif it war he.'

18.
    The king called on his merry men,
    By thirty and by three;
    Sweet Willie, wha used to be foremost man,
    Was the hindmost a' but three.

19.
    19.[2] 'twa-fald o'er a tree,' bent double on a stick.
    O he cam cripple, and he cam blind,
    Cam twa-fald o'er a tree:
    'O be he cripple, or be he blind,
    This very same man is he.'

20.
    'O whether will ye marry the bonny may,
    Or hang on the gallows-tree?'
    'O I will rather marry the bonny may,
    Afore that I do die.'

21.
    But he took out a purse of gold,
    Weel locked in a glove:
    'O tak ye that, my bonny may,
    And seek anither love.'

22.
    'O I will hae none o' your gold,' she says,
    'Nor as little ony of your fee,
    But I will hae your ain body,
    The king has granted me.'

23.
    O he took out a purse of gold;
    A purse of gold and store;
    'O tak ye that, fair may,' he said,
    'Frae me ye'll ne'er get mair.'

24.
    'O haud your tongue, young man,' she says,
    'And I pray you let me be;
    For I will hae your ain body,
    The king has granted me.'

25.
> He mounted her on a bonny bay horse,
> Himsel' on the silver grey;
> He drew his bonnet out o'er his een,
> He whipt and rade away.

26.
> 26.⁴ 'Sned,' cut, lop.
> O whan they cam to yon nettle bush,
> The nettles they war spread:
> 'O an my mither war but here,' she says,
> 'These nettles she wad sned.'

27.
> 'O an I had drank the wan water
> Whan I did drink the wine,
> That e'er a shepherd's dochter
> Should hae been a love o' mine!'

28.
> 'O may be I'm a shepherd's dochter,
> And may be I am nane!
> But you might hae ridden on your ways,
> And hae let me alane.'

29.
> 29.² Two lines wanting in the MS.
> O whan they cam unto yon mill
> She heard the mill clap:
>
> .   .   .   .   .
> .   .   .   .   .

30.
> 30.³ 'pock,' bag.
> 30.⁴ 'grey,' *i.e.* grey meal, barley.
> 'Clap on, clap on, thou bonny mill,
> Weel may thou, I say,
> For mony a time thou's filled my pock
> Wi' baith oat-meal and grey.'

31.
> 'O an I had drank the wan water
> Whan I did drink the wine,
> That e'er a shepherd's dochter
> Should hae been a love o' mine!'

32.
    'O may be I'm a shepherd's dochter,
    And may be I am nane;
    But you might hae ridden on your ways,
    And hae let me alane.

33.
    'But yet I think a fitter match
    Could scarcely gang thegither
    Than the King of France's auld dochter
    And the Queen of Scotland's brither.'

GET UP AND BAR THE DOOR

THE TEXT is from Herd's *Ancient and Modern Scots Songs* (1769), which is almost identical with a copy in Johnson's *Museum*. Another variant, also given in the *Museum*, was contributed by Burns, who made it shorter and more dramatic.

THE STORY of this farcical ballad has long been popular in many lands, European and Oriental, and has been introduced as an episode in English, French, and German plays. A close parallel to the ballad may be found in Straparola, Day VIII., first story.

GET UP AND BAR THE DOOR

1.
>   IT fell about the Martinmas time,
>   And a gay time it was then,
>   When our goodwife got puddings to make,
>   And she's boil'd them in the pan.

2.
>   The wind sae cauld blew south and north,
>   And blew into the floor;
>   Quoth our goodman to our goodwife,
>   'Gae out and bar the door.'

3.
>   3.[1] 'hussyfskep' = housewife's skep, a straw basket for meal.
>   'My hand is in my hussyfskep,
>   Goodman, as ye may see;
>   An it shoud nae be barr'd this hundred year,
>   It's no be barr'd for me.'

4.
>   They made a paction 'tween them twa,
>   They made it firm and sure,
>   That the first word whae'er shoud speak,
>   Shoud rise and bar the door.

5.
>   Then by there came two gentlemen,
>   At twelve o'clock at night,
>   And they could neither see house nor hall,
>   Nor coal nor candle-light.

6.

6.⁴ 'For,' *i.e.* to prevent: cp. *Child Waters*, 28.⁶ (First Series, p. 41).
'Now whether is this a rich man's house,
Or whether is it a poor?'
But ne'er a word wad ane o' them speak,
For barring of the door.

7.
And first they ate the white puddings,
And then they ate the black;
Tho' muckle thought the goodwife to hersel',
Yet ne'er a word she spake.

8.
Then said the one unto the other,
'Here, man, tak ye my knife;
Do ye tak aff the auld man's beard,
And I'll kiss the goodwife.'

9.
9.³ 'what ails ye,' etc. = why not use the pudding-broth.
'But there's nae water in the house,
And what shall we do than?'
'What ails ye at the pudding-broo,
That boils into the pan?'

10.
10.⁴ 'sca'd,' scald.
O up then started our goodman,
An angry man was he:
'Will ye kiss my wife before my een,
And sca'd me wi' pudding-bree?'

11.
Then up and started our goodwife,
Gi'ed three skips on the floor:
'Goodman, you've spoken the foremost word,
Get up and bar the door.'

END OF THE SECOND SERIES

APPENDIX

THE GREAT SILKIE OF SULE SKERRIE (p. 63)

SINCE the version given in the text was in type, my friend Mr. A. Francis Steuart of Edinburgh has kindly pointed out to me the following fuller and better variant of the ballad, which was unknown to Professor Child. It may be found in R. Menzies Fergusson's *Rambling Sketches in the Far North and Orcadian Musings* (1883), pp. 140-141, whence I have copied it, only adding the numbers to the stanzas.

THE GREY SELCHIE OF SHOOL SKERRY

1.
>IN Norway lands there lived a maid,
>'Hush, ba, loo lillie,' this maid began;
>'I know not where my baby's father is,
>Whether by land or sea does he travel in.'

2.
>It happened on a certain day,
>When this fair lady fell fast asleep,
>That in cam' a good grey selchie,
>And set him doon at her bed feet,

3.
>Saying, 'Awak', awak', my pretty fair maid.
>For oh! how sound as thou dost sleep!
>An' I'll tell thee where thy baby's father is;
>He's sittin' close at thy bed feet.'

4.
>'I pray, come tell to me thy name,
>Oh! tell me where does thy dwelling be?'
>'My name it is good Hein Mailer,
>An' I earn my livin' oot o' the sea.

5.
>'I am a man upon the land;
>I am a selchie in the sea;
>An' whin I'm far frae every strand,
>My dwellin' is in Shool Skerrie.'

6.
>'Alas! alas! this woeful fate!
>This weary fate that's been laid for me!

      That a man should come frae the Wast o' Hoy,
      To the Norway lands to have a bairn wi' me.'

7.
      'My dear, I'll wed thee with a ring,
      With a ring, my dear, I'll wed wi' thee.'
      'Thoo may go wed thee weddens wi' whom thoo wilt;
      For I'm sure thoo'll never wed none wi' me.'

8.
      'Thoo will nurse my little wee son
      For seven long years upo' thy knee,
      An' at the end o' seven long years
      I'll come back an' pay the norish fee.'

9.
      She's nursed her little wee son
      For seven long years upo' her knee,
      An' at the end o' seven long years
      He cam' back wi' gold an' white monie.

10.
      She says, 'My dear, I'll wed thee wi' a ring,
      With a ring, my dear, I'll wed wi' thee.'
      'Thoo may go wed thee weddens wi' whom thoo will;
      For I'm sure thoo'll never wed none wi' me.

11.
      'But I'll put a gold chain around his neck,
      An' a gey good gold chain it'll be,
      That if ever he comes to the Norway lands,
      Thoo may hae a gey good guess on hi'.

12.
      'An' thoo will get a gunner good,
      An' a gey good gunner it will be,
      An' he'll gae oot on a May mornin'
      An' shoot the son an' the grey selchie.'

13.
      Oh! she has got a gunner good,
      An' a gey good gunner it was he,
      An' he gaed oot on a May mornin',
      An' he shot the son and the grey selchie.

When the gunner returned from his expedition and showed the Norway woman the gold chain, which he had found round the neck of the young seal, the poor woman, realising that her son had perished, gives expression to her sorrow in the last stanza:—

14.
    'Alas! alas! this woeful fate!
    This weary fate that's been laid for me!'
    An' ance or twice she sobbed and sighed,
    An' her tender heart did brak in three.

    NOTE.—Doubtless *grey* selchie is more correct than *great*, as in the other version. Some verses were forgotten after stanza 13.

THE LYKE-WAKE DIRGE (p. 88)

'Art thow i-wont at lychwake

Any playes for to make?'

JOHN MYRC's Instructions for Parish Priests (circa 1450).

AUBREY's version of *The Lyke-Wake Dirge* is printed, more or less correctly, in the following places:—

i. Brand. *Observations on Popular Antiquities*, ed. Ellis (1813), ii. 180-81. (Not in first edition of Brand.)

ii. W. J. Thoms. *Anecdotes and Traditions*, Camden Society, 1839, pp. 88-90, and notes pp. 90-91, which are reprinted by Britten (see below).

iii. W. K. Kelly. *Curiosities of Indo-European Tradition and Folklore*, 1863, pp. 116-17.

iv. Edward Peacock. In notes, pp. 90-92, to John Myrc's *Instructions for Parish Priests*, E.E.T.S., 1868. (Re-edited by F. J. Furnivall for the E.E.T.S., 1902, where the notes are on pp. 92-94.)

v. James Britten. *Aubrey's Remains of Gentilisme and Judaisme*: the whole MS. edited for the Folklore Society, 1881, pp. 30-32.

Aubrey's remarks and sidenotes are as follow (Lansdowne MS. 231, fol. 114 *recto*):—

'From Mr. Mawtese, in whose father's youth, sc. about 60 yeares since now (1686), at country vulgar Funerals, was sung this song.

'At the Funeralls in Yorkeshire, to this day, they continue the custome of watching & sitting up all night till the body is inhersed. In the interim some kneel down and pray (by the corps) some play at cards some drink & take Tobacco: they have also Mimicall playes & sports, e.g. they choose a simple young fellow to be a Judge, then the suppliants (having first blacked their hands by rubbing it under the bottom of the Pott) beseech his Lo:p [*i.e.* Lordship] and smutt all his face. ['They play likewise at Hott-cockles.' — *Sidenote.*] Juvenal, Satyr II.

"Esse aliquos manes, et subterranea regna,

"Et contum, & Stygio ranas in gurgite nigras,

"Atq. unâ transire vadum tot millia cymbâ.

'This beliefe in Yorkshire was amongst the vulgar (& phaps is in part still) that after the persons death, the Soule went over Whinny moore ['Whin is a furze.' —*Sidenote*.] and till about 1616 (1624) at the Funerall a woman came [like a Præfica] and sung this following Song.'

Then follow several verses scratched out, and then the Dirge, to which, however, is prefixed the remark,

'This not ye first verse.'

As regards the doubtful reading 'sleete' for 'fleet,' there is curiously contradictory evidence. Pennant, in his *Tour in Scotland*, MDCCLXIX. (Chester, 1771, pp. 91-92), remarks:—

'On the death of a Highlander, the corps being stretched on a board, and covered with a coarse linen wrapper, the friends lay on the breast of the deceased a wooden platter, containing a small quantity of salt and earth, separate and unmixed; the earth, an emblem of the corruptible body; the salt, an emblem of the immortal spirit. All fire is extinguished where a corps is kept; and it is reckoned so ominous, for a dog or cat to pass over it, that the poor animal is killed without mercy.

'The *Late-wake* is a ceremony used at funerals: the evening after the death of any person, the relations and friends of the deceased meet at the house, attended by bagpipe or fiddle; the nearest of kin, be it wife, son, or daughter, opens a melancholy ball, dancing and greeting; *i.e.* crying violently at the same time; and this continues till daylight; but with such gambols and frolicks, among the younger part of the company, that the loss which occasioned them is often more than supplied by the consequences of that night. If the corps remains unburied for two nights the same rites are renewed.'

The Rev. J. C. Atkinson, on the other hand, states the contrary regarding the fire,—see his *Glossary of the Cleveland Dialect* (1868), p. 595. He supposes 'fleet' to be equivalent to the Cleveland 'flet,' live embers. 'The usage, hardly extinct even yet in the district, was on no account to suffer the fire in the house to go out during the entire time the corpse lay in it, and throughout the same time a candle was (or is yet) invariably kept burning in the same room with the corpse.'

Bishop Kennett, in Lansdowne MS. 1033, fol. 132, confirms Aubrey's gloss of 'fleet' = water, in quoting the first verse of the dirge. He adds, 'hence the *Fleet*, *Fleet-ditch*, in *Lond.* Sax. fleod, amnis, fluvius.'

The 'Brig o' Dread' (which is perhaps a corruption of 'the Bridge of the Dead'), 'Whinny-moor,' and the Hell-shoon, have parallels in many folklores. Thus, for the Brig, the Mohammedans have their *Al-Sirat*, finer than a hair, sharper than a razor, stretched over the midst of hell. The early Scandinavian mythology told of a bridge over the river Giöll on the road to hell.

In Snorri's *Edda*, when Hermôdhr went to seek the soul of Baldr, he was told by the keeper of the bridge, a maiden named Môdhgudhr, that the bridge rang beneath no feet save his. Similarly Vergil tells us that Charon's boat (which is also a parallel to the Brig) was almost sunk by the weight of Æneas.

Whinny-moor is also found in Norse and German mythology. It has to be traversed by all departed souls on their way to the realms of Hel or Hela, the Goddess of Death. These realms were not only a place of punishment: all who died went there, even the gods themselves taking nine days and nights on the journey. The souls of Eskimo travel to Torngarsuk, where perpetual summer reigns; but the way thither is five days' slide down a precipice covered with the blood of those who have gone before.

The passage of Whinny-moor or its equivalent is facilitated by Hell-shoon. These are obtained by the soul in various ways: the charitable gift of a pair of shoes during life assures the right to use them in crossing Whinny-moor; or a pair must be burned with the corpse, or during the wake. In one of his Dialogues, Lucian makes the wife of Eukrates return for the slipper which they had forgotten to burn.

Another parallel, though more remote, to the Hell-shoon, is afforded by the account of one William Staunton, who, like so many others, was privileged to see a vision of Purgatory and of the Earthly Paradise, on the first Friday after the feast of the Exaltation of the Cross in the year 1409. Accounts of such experiences, it may be remarked here, were popular from the tenth century onwards amongst the Anglo-Saxons and English, especially after the middle of the twelfth century, when the story of the famous 'St. Patrick's Purgatory' was first published. William Staunton relates (Royal MS. 17 B. xliii. in the British Museum) that in one part of Purgatory, as he went along the side of a 'water, the which was blak and fowle to sight,' he saw on the further side a tower, with a fair woman standing thereon, and a ladder against the tower: but 'hit was so litille, as me thowght that it wold onnethe [scarcely] bere ony thing; and the first rong of the ladder was so that onnethe might my fynger reche therto, and that rong was sharper than ony rasor.' Hearing a 'grisly noyse' coming towards him, William 'markid' himself with a prayer, and the noise vanished, and he saw a rope let down over the ladder from the top of the tower. And when the woman had drawn him safely to the top, she told him that the cord was one that he had once given to a chapman who had been robbed.

The whole subject of St. Patrick's Purgatory is extremely interesting; but it is outside our present scope, and can best be studied in connection with the mythology of the *Lyke-wake Dirge* in Thomas Wright's *St. Patrick's*

Purgatory (1844). The popularity of the story is attested by accounts extant in some thirty-five Latin and English MSS. in the British Museum, in the Bodleian, at Cambridge, and at Edinburgh. Calderon wrote a drama round the myth, *El Purgatorio de San Patricio*; Robert Southey a ballad; and an early poem of George Wither's, lost in MS., treated of the same subject. Recently the tale has received attention in G. P. Krapp's *Legend of St. Patrick's Purgatory*, Baltimore, 1900.

A correspondent in *Notes and Queries*, 9th Ser., xii. 475 (December 12, 1903), remarks that the 'liche-wake' is still spoken of in the Peak district of Derbyshire.

CPSIA information can be obtained
at www.ICGtesting.com
Printed in the USA
LVHW110851190521
687790LV00006B/244